SIX ESSAYS
ON
ERASMUS

SIX ESSAYS ON
ERASMUS

AND A TRANSLATION OF
ERASMUS' LETTER TO
CARONDELET, 1523

John C. Olin

NEW YORK
FORDHAM UNIVERSITY PRESS
1979

© Copyright 1979 by FORDHAM UNIVERSITY PRESS
All rights reserved.
LC 76–18467
ISBN 0–8232–1023–5 (clothbound)
ISBN 0–8232–1024–3 (paperback)

Printed in the United States of America

TO
MARIAN

ABBREVIATIONS

Allen — *Opus epistolarum Des. Erasmi Roterodami.* Edd. P. S. Allen, H. M. Allen, and H. W. Garrod. 12 vols. Oxford, 1906–1958.

LB — *Erasmi Opera Omnia.* Ed. Johannes Clericus. 10 vols. Leiden, 1703–1706.

CWE — *Collected Works of Erasmus.* In progress. Toronto and Buffalo, 1974—.

CHR — *Christian Humanism and the Reformation: Selected Writings of Erasmus.* Ed. John C. Olin. New York, 1975.

CONTENTS

PREFACE

THESE ESSAYS are attempts at understanding Erasmus—his aims, his influence, his historical image. Erasmus' true face has always been difficult to delineate, and even in his own day he was the object of serious misunderstanding and contradictory appraisals. Professor Bainton has said that he "has never had his due." All will certainly not be righted in this slim book, nor will every question be answered or obscurity removed. Rather the intention has been to throw light on certain features of Erasmus, some of which have not always been cut in high relief, and to view a more authentic visage. My hope is that I have rendered him some small measure of his due.

The first essay is the most comprehensive. It explores the underlying purpose of Erasmus, the aim of his scholarship and his life's work, and it stresses that his main objective was religious reform. It describes very broadly the character and course of this steadfast endeavor. It may be said to strike the keynote for the other essays in the volume. The second essay focuses on a specific aspect of Erasmus' reform, namely his opposition to war and his concern for peace, and it views his pacifism as an integral part of his religious consciousness and his Christian humanism. The third essay discusses the largest and most important segment of Erasmus' scholarly work—his numerous editions of the early Church Fathers. It emphasizes the extent of his labor and the role it played in his effort to restore theology. The fourth essay examines Erasmus' famous book *The Praise of Folly* and seeks to explain the structural unity and clarify the meaning of this satiric work. The fifth essay deals with the interpretation of Erasmus by later historians and with the problem of understanding him and his position amid the controversies of his time. My last essay is centered on Ignatius Loyola, but it examines the correspondence between the thought and spirituality of Ignatius and that of Erasmus and suggests the possibility of the latter's influence on the founder of the Jesuits.

To these six essays has been added a translation of Erasmus' long letter to Jean de Carondelet of January 5, 1523 which served as the dedication and preface to his edition of the works of St. Hilary of Poitiers. Written as the religious controversy precipitated by Luther's Ninety-five Theses had led to widespread discord, and addressed to a high official at the Hapsburg court in the Low Countries, it is one of Erasmus' most important compositions—a major statement of his point of view as a humanist scholar and reformer now confronted by schism in the Church. This particular writing has never previously been published in English. I might also note that the actual copy of the 1523 Hilary edition which Erasmus sent to Carondelet is in Harvard's Houghton Library and that the title page of that copy bearing an inscription in Erasmus' bold hand is shown as an illustration in this volume. We have also used as an illustration to accompany this text a contemporary portrait of Carondelet currently in the collection of the Brooklyn Museum.

My purpose in assembling and presenting these essays including the prefatory letter in this volume is to make them available as a general introduction to Erasmus and his thought. They touch on many of his most important endeavors and concerns, and their themes are central both to his thought and to our own understanding of him. They do not, of course, exhaust the story of Erasmus whose personality had many facets, whose mind and pen were extremely prolific, and whose labors were enormous. To inspect even cursorily his extensive correspondence in P. S. Allen's magnificent edition is to realize how far and wide his net was cast. But these essays do, I trust, give a fair and substantial picture of the great humanist and of the cause he served. May they move the reader to further inquiry and a fuller acquaintance.

Four of my essays have appeared separately in various publications before. "Erasmus and Reform" was the introduction in *Christian Humanism and the Reformation: Selected Writings of Erasmus,* ed. John C. Olin (New York: Harper Torchbook, 1965; revised edition, New York: Fordham University Press, 1975). "The Pacifism of Erasmus" was published in the Fordham University Quarterly *Thought* in December 1975. "Interpreting Erasmus" appeared under the title "Erasmus and His Place in History" in *Erasmus of Rotterdam, A Quincentennial Symposium,* ed. Richard L. DeMolen (New York: Twayne, 1971). "Erasmus and St. Ignatius Loyola" was the concluding essay in *Luther, Erasmus and the Reformation: A Catholic–Protestant Reappraisal,* edd. John C. Olin, James D. Smart, and Robert E. McNally, s.j. (New York: Fordham University Press, 1969). Some revising has occurred, and postscripts to the last two essays have been added. The other two essays and the translation of the Erasmus text are making their debut here. I read the substance of "Erasmus and the Church Fathers," however, at the Sixteenth Century Studies Conference at the University of Iowa in October 1975, and I plan to produce eventually a more detailed study on this theme. The translation of the letter to Carondelet was the joint work of Professor James F. Brady of the Department of Classics of Fordham University and me. I want to take this opportunity to express my heartfelt thanks for his expert assistance and very generous collaboration.

JOHN C. OLIN

SIX ESSAYS
ON
ERASMUS

1

ERASMUS AND REFORM

Nomen Erasmi nunquam peribit: "The name of Erasmus will never perish." This imposing judgment passed in 1516 by the great English humanist John Colet may strike us as exaggerated today, for though Erasmus' name is still alive, the image evoked in most cases by his name is either that of the clever, irreverent author of *The Praise of Folly* or that of the fastidious and detached scholar suggested by Holbein's famous portrait in the Louvre. In both instances cleverness, sophistication, and the lack of serious commitment seem small grounds for immortality.

Perhaps Colet's judgment is too imposing, but at least it attests the fame and importance of Erasmus in his own times. And his eminence among his contemporaries can be explained quite simply: he was the greatest scholar and writer of his age, and the significance of his scholarly achievement as well as the sincerity and integrity of his moral purpose were recognized by his whole generation. He had his enemies, to be sure, but the best and the mightiest acclaimed his worth.

So concise an explanation, however, does not exhaust the subject of Erasmus' ascendancy. There are still the questions of knowing what it was he achieved or sought to achieve, and of understanding the reason for the influence he exerted. And there may also be some confusion about the respect and authority he commanded in his day, for not long after Colet's prophetic declaration Erasmus was caught in the religious conflict in the sixteenth century that embroiled all of Christendom, and he became for many an object of suspicion and attack.

In a short essay, or indeed in a single book, all the questions that arise concerning Erasmus' influence and career cannot be answered, but it is the objective here, in view of the esteem in which his contemporaries held him, to explore a cardinal one. What was it that Erasmus did or tried to do? What was the fundamental purpose of his endeavors, the aim of his life's work?

An earlier version of this essay appeared in *Christian Humanism and the Reformation: Selected Writings of Erasmus*, ed. John C. Olin (New York: Fordham University Press, 1975), pp. 1–21.

This is a basic question because obviously all of Erasmus' thought and action hinge upon it. To know his underlying intention, to know the purpose that moved him, is to understand in large measure what he did and what he wrote and what the role was that he played in the Europe of his time. Such a question of course assumes a unity and constancy of purpose on the part of Erasmus, but that assumption shall be made at the outset and justified or not in the pages that follow. In fact a constancy of purpose along with a consistency in the ideas he expressed may even be said to be one of the most striking features of Erasmus' thought. His age was an age of change and cataclysm, but throughout the many years of his active life he remained extraordinarily true to the vocation and the ideal he had set for himself in his early days.

This question of Erasmus' aim or goal must first be approached against the background of his early life. The main facts, drawn from his *Compendium vitae* and early correspondence, are clear enough. He was born in Rotterdam probably in the year 1466, and his birth was illegitimate. Raised by his mother, though his father, a priest, was apparently very solicitous about him and his education, he was sent to elementary school in Gouda and later to a famous school in Deventer staffed by the Brothers of the Common Life. His stay in Deventer warrants emphasis, for here in his truly formative years—from about 1475 to 1484—he made close contact with the *Devotio moderna*, that spirit and program of evangelical piety which characterized the work of the Brothers of the Common Life and which found its fullest expression in that great masterpiece of the spiritual life *The Imitation of Christ*. There he also gained an introduction to the new humanism or classical learning that was now making its appearance in northern Europe, for these years witnessed the expansion of that enthusiasm for the literature of antiquity and that attempt to recover and restore it in its fullness which hitherto had been confined to the scholars of Italy. A noted humanist, Alexander Hegius, became headmaster of the school toward the close of Erasmus' stay, and the most celebrated German humanist of the day, Rudolph Agricola, delivered a lecture at the school which made a deep impression on the youthful mind of Erasmus.

His education at Deventer ended with his mother's death, soon followed by his father's, and Erasmus came under the care of guardians, who first packed him off to a dismal school at 's Hertogenbosch and then induced him to enter the monastery of the Augustinian canons at Steyn. This last step came to be the cause of much regret and bitterness for Erasmus, though at the time he appears to have adapted himself to the monastic life without great difficulty. He took his solemn vows after a year (that is, around 1488), he continued to cultivate his now lively interest in the Latin classics and the new humanist scholarship, and in 1492 he was ordained a priest. Not long after this he obtained an appointment as a secretary to the bishop of Cambrai, an important personage in the Low Countries at this time, and Erasmus left his monastery and the confines of his native Holland to enter the wider world that now beckoned to his eager spirit.

He did not remain long in the service of the bishop of Cambrai. In 1495 he won his patron's consent to go to Paris, where he planned to study for his degree of doctor of theology. His experience at the University of Paris both appalled and repelled him. He saw nothing of value or virtue in the arid scholasticism to which he was exposed, and he became acutely aware of the contrast between the barren disputations of his present masters and the learning and eloquence of the ancients.[1] This aversion to the methods and practitioners of scholastic theology will find constant expression in the writings of Erasmus and is one of the keys to understanding his life's work.[2] However, all was not disappointment and pain in Paris, though it was on the whole a trying period of uncertainty and adjustment. He pursued his classical studies and entered the threshold of the Paris humanist circle. To support himself when aid from his bishop–patron proved inadequate, he tutored some well-to-do students in Latin literature and style. One of these was a young English noble, Lord Mountjoy, who invited Erasmus to visit England in the summer of 1499.

This visit, whose duration was about eight months, marks the turning point of his life. "He came there," writes Johan Huizinga, "as an erudite poet, the protégé of a nobleman of rank, on the road to closer contact with the great world which knew how to appreciate and reward literary merit. He left the country with the fervent desire in future to employ his gifts, in so far as circumstances would permit, in more serious tasks. This change was brought about by two new friends, whose personalities were far above those who had hitherto crossed his path: John Colet and Thomas More."[3]

Up to this time Erasmus was searching his way. Classical letters had more and more absorbed his interest, and this in turn had led to his departure from the monastery at Steyn and to his rejection of the scholasticism he encountered in Paris. His future, however, was not resolved, nor was his purpose clear. In England he found his bearings. There he met men whose learning tremendously impressed him and whose character and religious devotion he could respect. He saw, moreover, a union established between a humanist enlightenment and an authentic Christian purpose. In this the example and friendship of Colet were of the utmost importance. Colet was lecturing on the Epistles of St. Paul at Oxford at this time and was using the grammatical and historical methods of the humanists to blaze a new path in theological study.[4] In him the exciting possibilities of a humanism scriptural and Christian came alive, and Erasmus, child of the *Devotio moderna* that he was but revolted by the stagnant religious culture he had come to know, saw what his own task must be. Colet tried to persuade Erasmus to lecture on the Old Testament at Oxford, a companion work to his own lectures on the New; but Erasmus, conscious of his present inadequacy, refused the invitation. It is clear, nevertheless, that Erasmus then, or very soon afterward, set the goal which would henceforth give direction to his life's work. This goal was, to put it succinctly, to employ humanism in the service of religion: that is, to apply the new scholarship to the study and understanding of Holy Scripture and thereby to restore theology and revivify religious life.

Erasmus returned to Paris in early 1500, and then began that great career which continued with unusual dedication and singleness of mind down to his death in 1536, and carried him to a pinnacle of influence attained by few other writers or scholars in European history. It was a life of intense scholarly and literary activity, comparable, in his own view, to the labors of Hercules. It was a restless life, marked by frequent travel and change of residence. Paris, Louvain, Venice, Cambridge, Basel, Freiburg—all became his temporary home. His books and editions poured forth, his fame grew, he carried on an enormous correspondence with the great and learned of his day, he saw to his sorrow Europe torn by bitter religious argument, and he witnessed the early consequences of what he had come to call "the Lutheran tragedy."[5] But withal he remained faithful to the cause of Christian learning which Colet had inspired.

Shortly after his return to Paris in 1500 Erasmus published his first and one of his most popular works, the *Adagia*, a collection of eight hundred short excerpts and proverbs from the Latin classics for those who would increase their classical knowledge and improve their Latin style. But this kind of improvement was no longer Erasmus' primary concern. He was now engaged in the study of Greek, which he viewed as an essential preparation for the study of Scripture, and conjointly he was absorbed in the correction and editing of the letters of St. Jerome, whom he had long cherished as a Christian scholar.[6] We have a most revealing letter from Erasmus to a close friend in Flanders at this time, in which he tells of his great design, his *magnum quiddam*, "to restore the whole Jerome as great as it is, corrupted, mutilated, confused by the ignorance of the theologians," and he links this important project to the restoration of true theology, *vera theologia*.[7] It is clear that in his mind Greek and Jerome were the means toward reopening Scripture itself and that on this kind of scholarship the true theology must be based.

In the fall of 1501 Erasmus interrupted these scholarly pursuits to write a moral treatise, a guide to Christian living, which is of the greatest importance in understanding the orientation and development of his thought. In this treatise, *Enchiridion militis christiani* (*The Handbook of the Christian Soldier*), the gulf is bridged between the academic endeavors which now absorbed him and the reform of Christian life which became his constant concern. Scholarship, classical, scriptural, and patristic, was not to be an end in itself but was to conduct men to a better life. Learning was to lead to virtue, scholarship to God, and thus, as Erasmus saw it, the restoration of theology was to be the means toward the revival of a living and lived Christianity. It is here that we come to the core of "the Erasmian idea," to the essential meaning of that Christian humanism whose greatest apostle Erasmus was. And in the *Enchiridion*, written at the outset of his career, we have the program he will henceforth follow.

Erasmus composed the *Enchiridion* ostensibly for a soldier who he was afraid might fall among "the superstitious kind of religious" that would drive him into "a sort of Judaism, and teach him not to love but to fear."[8] Developing the theme that life is a constant warfare against sin, he explains the weapons that the Christian must employ and the rules and precepts that must guide him in his unending struggle. Two fundamental and related ideas run throughout the book. One is that the great weapon of the Christian is the knowledge of Holy Scripture; the other is that religion consists primarily not of outward signs and devotions but of the inward love of God and neighbor. This latter idea is particularly emphasized—it will become Erasmus' master thought—and some of the most striking and characteristic passages of the *Enchiridion* express it:

> You venerate saints; you are glad to touch their relics. But you contemn what good they have left, namely the example of a pure life. No worship of Mary is more gracious than if you imitate Mary's humility. No devotion to the saints is more acceptable and more proper than if you strive to express their virtue. You wish to deserve well of Peter and Paul? Imitate the faith of one, the charity of the other—and you will hereby do more than if you were to dash back and forth to Rome ten times. . . . And although an example of universal piety be sought most fittingly from Christ, yet if the worship of Christ in his saints delights you very much, imitate Christ in the saints, and to the honor of each one change one vice, or be zealous to embrace a particular virtue. If this happens, I will not disapprove those things which are now done in public.[9]

Or again:

> Do not tell me therefore that charity consists in being frequently in church, in prostrating oneself before signs of the saints, in burning tapers, in repeating such and such a number of prayers. God has no need of this. Paul defines love as: to edify one's neighbor, to lead all to become members of the same body, to consider all one in Christ, to rejoice concerning a brother's good fortune in the Lord just as concerning your own, to heal his hurt just as your own.[10]

This of course is a rule—*the* rule—for the Christian life which Erasmus draws from Scripture, and he urges his friend to the zealous study of the word of God. He suggests that some of the pagan authors may be read as a preliminary training, "for they are often good moral teachers," and he recommends the Platonists because "they approach as closely as possible the prophetic and Gospel pattern."[11] However, Holy Scripture "divinely inspired and perfected by God its Author"[12] is pre-eminent, and there is never a question in the *Enchiridion* (or any place else in Erasmus) of reducing Christianity to a level with paganism or of creating some kind of naturalistic religious synthesis. There is sometimes a misunderstanding of Erasmus on this score, but even a cursory reading of his works, it would seem, must dispel it.[13]

In the interpretation of Scripture he commends the ancient Fathers—Origen, Ambrose, Jerome, Augustine—and he warns against the modern theologians, those *neoterici,* who drink in the letter of the Sacred Writings but not the spirit, or who rely on Duns Scotus and fail to read Scripture itself.[14] "Especially make yourself familiar with Paul," he exhorts in his famous closing passage, wherein he also reveals that he has been working on a commentary on St. Paul and for that purpose has studied ancient literature and acquired a knowledge of Greek and Latin:

> We have not undertaken their study for empty fame or childish pleasure of mind, but long ago put our mind to it that we might with exotic riches abundantly adorn the Lord's temple (which some persons have too much dishonored out of their own ignorance and barbarousness). By these efforts the generous natural qualities can be kindled to the love of divine Scripture.[15]

One other feature stands out most forcefully in reading the *Enchiridion,* and that is Erasmus' emphasis on the mystical body of Christ. He is constantly calling his reader's attention to the fact that he is a brother to his neighbor, a member of the same body whose head is Christ:

It is not the Christian's way to reason thus: "What have I to do with him? I know not whether he be white or black, he is unknown, he is a stranger, he never deserved anything well of me." . . . Consider this: he is your brother in the Lord, coheir with you in Christ, a member of the same body, redeemed by the same blood, a comrade in the common faith, called to the same grace and happiness in the future life.[16]

This concept, which Erasmus roots firmly in the great Pauline texts, inspires most of his moral injunctions and forms the basis of what we may call, for want of a better term, his social outlook. He is led thereby to denounce the selfishness, the indifference, the greed that contribute to the ills and injustices of the world:

Your brother needs your help, but you meanwhile mumble your little prayers to God, pretending not to see your brother's need.[17]

You gamble away a thousand pieces of gold in one night, while some poor girl, plunged into dire need, prostitutes her body and loses her soul, for which Christ poured out his soul. You say: "What has that to do with me? My own concerns take up all my thoughts." And afterwards will you see yourself a Christian with this mind, who may not even be a man? . . . The law punishes you if you take unto yourself what belongs to another. It does not punish you, if you take your possessions away from a needy brother. Yet even so Christ will punish you.[18]

He is also led to deplore disunity and dissension among Christians and its most terrible manifestation—war. It remains for his later writings to express more fully the social application of the scriptural message, particularly on the subject of dissension and war,[19] but there is no mistaking his realization of this application in the pages of the *Enchiridion*. In brief, Erasmus was already keenly aware of the relevance of Christianity to the problems of his day.

Erasmus thus emerges, as he begins those labors which thereafter will engage him, as a reformer—a reformer of theology, a reformer of morals, a reformer of society. The three spheres are intimately connected. The advance of humanist scholarship and the expansion of Christian knowledge are the means whereby the needed reforms will come. He is aware of the limitations of human learning, yet it is knowledge, not ignorance, that will reveal God's truth and God's way. His lifelong efforts are posited on that belief.

Practically the whole corpus of Erasmus' work can be interpreted in this light. Certainly a brief consideration of the important writings and editions of Erasmus will surely bear this out and indicate as well both the later development of his reform program and the continuity of his thought. In this connection one cannot fail to speak of Erasmus' best known and most widely read book, *The Praise of Folly*. This little masterpiece, quite unlike anything else Erasmus ever wrote, was dashed off in 1509 at Thomas More's house in London, where Erasmus was recuperating after a long stay in Italy and an arduous journey back to England.[20] It is a book which lends itself to varying interpretations, for it is a kind of seriocomic joke, expressing frequently the most outrageous things; yet, as its first English translator observed, in every sentence, "almost in every clause, is hidden, besides the mirth, some deeper sense and purpose."[21] This deeper sense and purpose, in perfect accord with the spirit of the *Enchiridion*, are simply to reveal the sham and hypocrisy of human affairs and to recall men to that higher folly of which St. Paul speaks, the folly of the Christian. Erasmus does this, however, not in the straightforward way of the moral teacher, as in the *Enchiridion*, although there are passages that are straightforward enough in *The Praise of Folly*, but with the wit, the irony, and the guile of a mischievous jester. The book therefore is subject to certain confusions and misunderstandings, and readers have frequently been shocked at what they consider the rejection of sanity or the mockery of sacred things. Actually, as Bouyer has pointed out, Erasmus "is simply laughing at humbug."[22]

Perhaps the most famous and remembered parts of *The Praise of Folly* are Erasmus' thrusts at religious superstitions and at the theologians, the monks, and the prelates who disfigure religion with their conceits and unchristian lives.[23] These occupy a fair portion of the book, and it is here that it has its most cutting effect. The theologians, as we might expect, are given some rough treatment. They are in the vanguard of the followers of Folly, who is personified in the book and who speaks throughout, and, wrapped in their syllogisms and self-pride, they are far removed from the spirit of the Gospels or Epistles, which moreover "they have no time to open."

> Next to the theologians in happiness are those who commonly call themselves "the religious" and "monks." Both are complete misnomers, since most of them stay as far away from religion as possible, and no people are seen more often in public. . . . They are so detested that it is considered bad luck if one crosses your path, and yet they are highly pleased with themselves. They cannot read, and so they consider it the height of piety to have no contact with literature. . . . Most of them capitalize on their dirt and poverty by whining for food from door to door. They push into inns, ships, and public conveyances, to the great disadvantage of the regular

beggars. These smooth fellows simply explain that by their very filth, ignorance, boorishness, and insolence they enact the lives of the apostles for
us. . . . They forget that Christ will condemn all of this and will call for a
reckoning of that which He has prescribed, namely, charity.[24]

These are strong words, but Erasmus, speaking through the mouth of
Folly, has reserved even stronger ones for unworthy popes. It is clear that
he has in mind the pontiff then reigning, Julius II, the warrior pope whom
he had recently seen in action in strife-torn Italy.

They fight for these things [i.e., the possessions of the Church] with fire
and sword, inflamed by Christian zeal, and not without shedding Christian blood. They look upon themselves as true apostles, defending the
bride of Christ, and scattering what they are pleased to call her enemies.
As if the church had more deadly enemies than impious popes who by
their silence cause Christ to be forgotten, who use His laws to make
money, who adulterate His word with forced interpretations, and who
crucify Him with their corrupt life.[25]

This piercing thrust at the pope who was then at the helm of the Church
leads immediately into one of Erasmus' first great condemnations of war
—a pursuit which he rejected as the very antithesis of the doctrine of Christ,
who had called us all to be one:

War is so monstrous a thing that it befits beasts and not men, so violently
insane that poets represent it as an evil visitation of the Furies, so pestilen-
tial that it causes a general corruption of character, so criminal that it is
best waged by the worst men, and so impious that it has no relation with
Christ. Nevertheless, our popes neglect everything else to devote themselves to war. . . . I can't decide [he humorously concludes] whether the
German bishops taught the popes all this, or whether it was the other
way around.[26]

The impact of *The Praise of Folly* was, and still is, considerable; but
for its proper evaluation it must be read and understood in the light of
certain facts. First, it is a particular and unusual kind of book, actually a
fool's book—and fools, as Erasmus points out, can get away with mur-
der.[27] Then the general context of its composition must be borne in mind.
It was written in 1509 in a Europe still Catholic though desperately in
need of religious reform.[28] Finally, Erasmus' deeper purpose must be
grasped: this is, not simply to criticize the follies and evils of mankind but
to amend a troubled world. Nowhere in *The Praise of Folly* does Erasmus
actually attack the doctrines and institutions of the Church, but only those
who, in his mind, have degraded and disfigured them. "Nor did I have

any intentions in the *Folly*," he himself wrote to his Louvain critic Martin Dorp, "different from those in my other works, although the method may have differed."[29]

The year 1516 is a memorable one in the story of Erasmus. In that year Erasmus completed and published his most widely heralded scholarly work, a Greek and Latin edition of the New Testament. That same year his publisher, Johann Froben of Basel, brought out his corrected edition of St. Jerome in nine volumes.[30] Both projects had been in preparation for many years, and their appearance may be said to mark the climax of Erasmus' career. His fame, his prestige, his influence now reached their height, and scholars everywhere acclaimed themselves *Erasmiani*—a term, by the way, which Erasmus reproved, for "we are all followers of Christ, and to His glory we all drudge, each for his part."[31] That same year he wrote his most important political treatise, *Institutio principis christiani* (*The Education of a Christian Prince*), dedicated to the young prince who would soon become Emperor Charles V, in which he counseled that "the teachings of Christ apply to no one more than to the prince."[32] And a few months later he wrote his great denunciation of war, *Querela pacis* (*The Complaint of Peace*), a remarkable document motivated by the most fervent Christian ideals but at the same time attuned to the circumstances and problems of his age.[33] It is hardly necessary to point out that in these works, as in his whole moral approach, Erasmus stands in striking contrast to another contemporary scholar and observer, Niccolò Machiavelli, whose own famous book *Il Principe* (*The Prince*) had been penned just a few years before. But if this contrast is exceedingly sharp, the similarity between the ideas of Erasmus and those expressed by Thomas More in *Utopia*, that supreme masterpiece of the Christian Renaissance, is very close. And 1516 is also the year of *Utopia*.

1516 then was a year of achievement for Erasmus and his friends, and hope in the eventual triumph of their reform ideas ran high. Peace now reigned in Europe, new and promising young princes were at the helm in the great Christian states, and a new birth of learning seemed about to crown an era of universal concord. The golden age anticipated by the humanists, however, was not to be. In March 1517 Giovanni Francesco Pico della Mirandola at a closing session of the Lateran Council in Rome warned the assembled Fathers that if Pope Leo failed to heal the wounds of the Church like a good physician with lancet and lint, God himself would cleanse those wounds with fire and sword.[34] That terrifying prophecy soon came true. In the fall of 1517 Luther advanced to the center of the stage, and the high drama of religious revolt and disruption began. Erasmus henceforth was caught in the headlong rush of events, and his figure was overshadowed by the more vehement actors that now dominated the scene. He did not disappear into the wings. He remained active to the end, his authority still unrivalled in the learned world; but what he achieved or sought to achieve became now of lesser moment than the grave issues Luther raised. The hope, too, of the reform of Christian life and society within the traditional frame of Christendom, as Erasmus envisaged it, was soon dashed to the ground.

The relation of Erasmus to the Protestant Reformation, particularly to its causation—did he "lay the egg Luther hatched"?[35]—is a broad and somewhat equivocal question upon which a consideration of his work can unquestionably shed some light. There is an obvious connection between the biblical humanism represented by Erasmus and the theological approach of Luther. The two, however, should not be identified, for it is just as obvious that Erasmus' understanding of Scripture (and his attitude toward the Church) differed essentially from the convictions of the early Protestant leaders.[36] Nor should too great stress be laid on Erasmus' influence as a critic and a reformer in the causal background of Protestantism. Both Erasmian reform and Protestantism are symptomatic, so to speak, of many of the same conditions in the Church and in the religious life of the time. They respond to many of the same abuses, but their responses are basically divergent, despite some resemblance on certain points of criticism and on certain theological tendencies. The letter Erasmus wrote to Jodocus Jonas in May 1521 is very instructive in this regard.[37] Erasmus opposed, both in their essence and in their effects, the "extreme remedies" which Luther now propounded.

It must also be acknowledged that Protestantism has a theological origin and doctrinal base quite distinct from Erasmian humanism. Therefore, to make Erasmus responsible in some way for Luther is to fail to do justice to both the unique role of Luther himself and Protestantism's own historic *raison d'être*. And it is to imply as well that Erasmus' cry for reform necessarily led to the disruption of the Church. There was indeed an historic nexus between reform and disruption in the sixteenth century, but that link will not be found in the thought and work of Erasmus.

It is true that in the beginning Erasmus had a certain sympathy for Luther and felt that the source of his action, rash though in some respects he might deem it to be, lay in those evils and abuses in the life of the Church which he himself had so long criticized and condemned.[38] He saw, too, that many of Luther's critics and opponents were men whom he

abhorred and who had in turn attacked his work, and he feared that their
victory in the Lutheran quarrel would embolden them in their resistance
to reform and enlightenment in general. But this initial approach must
be examined carefully in its context, and one must especially bear in mind
Erasmus' aim of working for reform within the framework of the Church.
As the controversy involving Luther became more vehement and widespread, he indeed became alarmed about its eventual outcome. In late 1520
he observed with considerable prescience that "the case was tending toward
a greater crisis than certain men suppose,"[39] and he began then to see it
as taking on the proportions of a "tragedy," a great disaster. Yet he still
sought to moderate the quarrel, to conciliate the factions, to prevent a
serious breach within the Church—or at least this remained the bent of
his mind and the natural direction of his efforts. He failed. And history
seldom bestows its accolade on those who fail, but it is his endeavor that
we seek to measure today.

By 1524 the time for compromise had passed, and Erasmus, pressed by
many to write authoritatively against Luther, composed and published
a significant work. This was his treatise *De libero arbitrio* (*On Free Will*),
in which he rejected one of Luther's fundamental teachings in the name
of Holy Scripture and man's own obligation to lead a moral life.[40] Up-
braiding Luther for his intemperance and excesses and for arguing so
dogmatically against all the Fathers, the councils, and the popes, he asserted a stand on the difficult problem of free will and grace that is clearly
in the Catholic tradition. The debate that followed was sharp and extensive, but Erasmus' primary concern nevertheless remained the reform of
Christian life and practice in the Church, and he continued to work with
all his energies toward that goal. "To refuse to remedy [the state of affairs
in the Church] in order the better to refute the Lutherans, was, in his
opinion, to cut the weed but leave its root," observes Bouyer.[41]

All through the 1520s he labored on new scholarly editions of the writings of the Fathers—Cyprian, Hilary, Irenaeus, Ambrose, Augustine, John
Chrysostom—and at the time of his death in 1536 he was completing an
edition of Origen, his favorite among the Greeks. He also wrote many
moral and religious treatises—and in these years appeared numerous editions of his *Colloquies*, his most famous book after *The Praise of Folly*.[42]
In this work, which consists *in toto* of some fifty short dialogues or con-
versations, we find much of the same wit and satire as in *The Praise of
Folly* together with those familiar and characteristic themes he had expressed as early as 1501 in the *Enchiridion*: the emphasis on Holy Scripture as the wellspring of Christian piety, the need for a life of simple faith

and charity as opposed to a life of external devotions alone, the rejection of sham and pretentiousness in religious practice, the obligation to aid the poor, the revulsion at war.

There is another theme prominent in the *Colloquies* which also deserves mention: namely, the way in which the Christian should face death. In "The Shipwreck" Erasmus tells the story of a ship caught and destroyed in a terrible storm. All on board are panic-stricken and in their distraught state scream to the saints for help and make extravagant vows. A young mother, with her child in her arms, alone retains her calm and dignity and prays in silence—and she is one of the very few who are saved. Again, in "The Religious Banquet," one of Erasmus' greatest colloquies, the attitude of Socrates in the face of death is discussed. His resignation and hope, so proper to the Christian, inspires Erasmus' interlocutor to utter these frequently quoted words: "I can hardly help exclaiming, 'Saint Socrates, pray for us.' "[43]

This theme may be an appropriate one on which to close this essay. As he tried to teach men how to live, so Erasmus also attempted to show them how to die. And he did this in the spirit that characterizes all his work—the spirit of evangelical simplicity which only the humblest and the wisest possess. The goal of Erasmus unquestionably was reform—the reform of theology through a return to Scripture and the reform of Christian life and society as the consequence of a scriptural revival. But behind this broad purpose it is the return to the honesty and simplicity of the Gospels that is the ever dominant note. It is in this cause basically that the son of the *Devotio moderna* employed his learning and his humanism. And in this perspective the young Christian mother and the Socrates of the *Colloquies* become figures of considerable significance in grasping the purpose of Erasmus.

A French scholar, Gentian Hervet, who had studied in England and who served as a tutor in the Pole family, in 1526 translated into English a sermon of Erasmus', "On the Mercy of God." In his preface to the sermon Hervet has this to say in praise of his author:

He is the man to whom in learning no living man may himself compare. . . . He is the man that to Isaac may be compared, the which digged up the goodly springing wells that the Philistines destroyed and with dirt and dung overfilled. The clear springs of Holy Scripture that the Philistines had so troubled, so marred, and so defiled, that no man could drink or have the true taste of the water, they be now by his labor and diligence to their old pureness and clearness so restored that no spot nor earthly filth in them remaineth.[44]

And it was for this reason that Colet had said that the name of Erasmus would never perish.

NOTES

1. See Erasmus' letter to Thomas Grey, August 1497. Allen, I, 190–97, and CWE, I, 135–38.

2. Denys Gorce, "La Patristique dans la réforme d'Erasme," *Festgabe Joseph Lortz* (Baden-Baden, 1958), I, 233ff., gives some interesting background relevant to late scholasticism and Erasmus' aversion to it.

3. J. Huizinga, *Erasmus of Rotterdam* (New York, 1952; Harper Torchbook edition, 1957, under the title *Erasmus and the Age of Reformation*), p. 29.

4. On Colet and his influence on Erasmus, see E. H. Harbison, *The Christian Scholar in the Age of the Reformation* (New York, 1956), pp. 55ff., and Frederic Seebohm, *The Oxford Reformers* (London, 1869). Erasmus' own biographical sketch of Colet is in the second letter to Jodocus Jonas, in CHR, Chap. IX.

5. This term, used frequently by Erasmus, is found as early as May 1521 in the preface written for his *Epistolae ad diversos*. Allen, IV, 499. The expression is also found in the *Compendium vitae* (CHR, Chap. I).

6. Allen, II, 210.

7. Letter to James Batt, c. December 12, 1500. Allen, I, 325–29, and CWE, I, 300–6.

8. Erasmus, *The Enchiridion*, trans. Ford Lewis Battles, in *Advocates of Reform from Wyclif to Erasmus*, ed. Matthew Spinka (London, 1953), p. 378. On the circumstances that prompted Erasmus to write the *Enchiridion*, see Allen, I, 19–20. The *Enchiridion* was first published in Antwerp in 1503.

9. Erasmus, *The Enchiridion*, pp. 337–38.

10. *Ibid.*, p. 345.

11. *Ibid.*, pp. 304–5.

12. *Ibid.*, p. 303.

13. See Louis Bouyer, *Erasmus and His Times* (Westminster, Md., 1959), pp. 161–64.

14. Erasmus, *The Enchiridion*, pp. 305–6, 334.

15. *Ibid.*, p. 379.

16. *Ibid.*, pp. 358–59.

17. *Ibid.*, p. 320.

18. *Ibid.*, pp. 360–61.

19. See Chapter 2, below.

20. See Chapter 4, below.

21. Sir Thomas Chaloner's introduction to his English translation, published in 1549, in *The Thought and Culture of the English Renaissance*, ed. E. M. Nugent (Cambridge, 1956), p. 59.

22. Bouyer, op. cit., p. 100.

23. Erasmus, *The Praise of Folly*, trans. Leonard F. Dean (Chicago, 1946), pp. 79–82, 95–104, 109–13.

24. *Ibid.*, pp. 101–2.

25. *Ibid.*, p. 112.

26. *Ibid.*, pp. 112–13.

27. *Ibid.*, p. 75.

28. Erasmus is very conscious of this time element in the subsequent appraisal of what he had written. See Allen, IV, 499. He comments on this situation in a letter to Jodocus Jonas, May 10, 1521 (CHR, Chap. VIII), declaring that if he had foreseen what was coming, he would not have written certain things or he would have written them in a different way. Beatus Rhenanus in his life of Erasmus (CHR, Chap. II) also reports that Erasmus often told him the same thing.

29. CHR, p. 59.

30. See Chapter 3, below.

31. Huizinga, op. cit., pp. 98–99.

32. Erasmus, *The Education of a Christian Prince*, trans. Lester K. Born (New York, 1936), p. 148. On Erasmus' political thought, see Pierre Mesnard, *L'Essor de la philosophie politique au XVIe siècle* (Paris, 1936), chap. II.

33. Erasmus, *The Complaint of Peace*, introd. William J. Hirten (New York, 1946). See also Chapter 2, below.

34. Pierre Janelle, *The Catholic Reformation* (Milwaukee, 1949), p. 45.

35. This is a contemporary charge attributed to the Franciscans of Cologne by Erasmus in a letter of December 1524. Allen, V, 609.

36. The theological disagreement between Erasmus and Luther goes back as far as 1516. In October of that year Luther wrote Spalatin that he disagreed with Erasmus' understanding of St. Paul, a matter that was communicated to Erasmus by Spalatin in a letter in December. Allen, II, 415–18. And in March 1517 Luther wrote to his close friend John Lang: "My opinion of Erasmus decreases from day to day. . . . I fear that he does not promote the cause of Christ and God's grace sufficiently. For him human considerations have an absolute preponderance over divine." Quoted in Heinrich Boehmer, *Martin Luther: Road to Reformation* (New York, 1957), p. 160. See also Harbison, op. cit., pp. 105–6.

37. See CHR, Chap. VIII.

38. See Erasmus' letter to Albert of Brandenburg, October 19, 1519 (CHR, Chap. VI). For an excellent review of Erasmus' relations with Luther and Lutheranism, see C. R. Thompson's introduction to his edition of Erasmus' *Inquisitio de fide* (New Haven, 1950).

39. CHR, p. 147.

40. Erasmus–Luther, *Discourse on Free Will*, trans. E. F. Winter (New York, 1961).

41. Bouyer, op. cit., p. 192. See also Myron Gilmore, *Humanists and Jurists* (Cambridge, Mass., 1963), Chap. V, for an excellent analysis of Erasmus' position and attitude in his later years.

42. *The Colloquies of Erasmus*, trans. C. R. Thompson (Chicago, 1965).

43. *Ibid.*, p. 68.

44. Nugent, op. cit., p. 349.

2

THE PACIFISM OF ERASMUS

THERE ARE SOME LINES IN RABELAIS which can be applied quite appropriately to Erasmus. They come at the end of *Gargantua* in the final chapter
where Rabelais gives us the strange enigmatic prophecy that was un-
earthed in digging the foundations of the abbey of Thélème. The prophecy
foretells the coming of strife and discord and profound turmoil on this
globe, this "round machine," as Rabelais calls it, but the recital of impend-
ing disaster is interrupted and relieved by a salute to those who work to
save the world and bring it peace.

> The happiest those who value her the most,
> And best abstain from damage and destruction,
> Attempting in whatever ways they can
> To master her and hold her prisoner
> In such a place that she, poor ruined globe,
> Shall turn for help only to Him that made her.[1]

The prophecy is subject to various interpretations and its very authorship
is a question, but the words just quoted can be said to describe in a striking way the role and aim of Erasmus amidst the contention and conflict
he witnessed in the Europe of his day. It was also, of course, the Europe
of Rabelais, and Erasmus was his master, nowhere more perhaps than
in the vision of the utopian abbey of Thélème, to which the enigmatic
prophecy is appended.[2] Rabelais, however, is not our main concern. These
lines from *Gargantua* are relevant because they evoke the peacemaking
efforts of Erasmus and suggest their context and their worth. They may
serve too as a tribute to the great Christian humanist.

To call Erasmus a great Christian humanist is to have in mind his pre-
eminence in the early sixteenth century in the European-wide movement
to reform Christian learning and Christian life by a return to the sources
of Europe's faith. The endeavor is humanist because it embraces the classical heritage and employs the method and approach of the Italian scholars

---

An earlier version of this essay appeared in *Thought*, Vol. 50, No. 199 (December 1975), 418–31.

of the Renaissance and because it has its origin and its model in the work
of these Italian scholars. It is Christian because its essential purpose and
preoccupation are religious and because its major contribution is a vast
literature of texts, commentaries, and other writings relevant to Christianity and inspired principally by the desire to rejuvenate, rekindle, and
apply it. Erasmus' publication in 1516 of his annotated Greek and Latin
New Testament and of a nine-volume edition of the letters and works of
St. Jerome is the high point of this movement. He does not, of course,
stand alone in this enterprise, but he is its exemplar and its most important
representative, and his career, extending from his first book, the *Adages*,
in 1500 to his death in 1536, is a monument of labor and dedication to this
cause. The high merit of his work, the wit and grace of his style, and his
incredible productivity won him a stature and influence achieved by few
others in European history.

There is also another significance in calling Erasmus a Christian humanist. This lies in the fact that he saw Christianity as in accord with
human nature, not in opposition to it, as completing and crowning the
work of creation as well as man's own achievement, not rejecting or dis-
placing the world of nature and the world of man. He should not be misunderstood on this score. He is not advancing, as some have thought, a
diluted Christianity or a neo-pagan naturalism. His synthesis is, to use
Henri de Lubac's term, a "converted humanism." He always sees man in
Christian terms, yet man himself has intrinsic value and potential, and
his culture is not a matter of aversion and disdain. Such a perspective is
firmly within the Christian tradition, and it has its counterpart, not to say
its source, in the early Fathers and in medieval thought.[3] For example,
when Erasmus wrote in his *Enchiridion militis christiani* that "any truth
you come upon is Christ's," he is actually repeating what Justin Martyr
had said in the second century, St. Augustine in the fourth, and St. Thomas
Aquinas in the thirteenth, and he is proclaiming what Etienne Gilson has
called "the perpetual charter of Christian humanism."[4] The more famous
exclamation of Erasmus, "Saint Socrates, pray for us," is but another way
of stating this recurrent theme, and it is interesting to note that this memorable expression is preceded in the colloquy where it appears by a discussion on how Christians can learn and profit from many of the works
of the ancient pagans.[5] "Perhaps the spirit of Christ is more widespread
than we understand," Erasmus observes.

This same openness and breadth of view can also be found in the *Paraclesis*, Erasmus' introduction to the Greek and Latin New Testament he
published in 1516, and there too is found another very important aspect of

his Christian humanism. Discussing "the philosophy of Christ" which he sees "in especial accord with human nature," Erasmus asks: "What else is the philosophy of Christ, which He himself calls a rebirth, than the restoration of human nature originally well formed?"[6] This statement reiterating the most ancient and traditional concept of Christian renewal bridges the gap between grace and nature, between Christ and the world, and unites these two orders in a relationship, the harmony of which is the very essence of Christian humanism. Christ alone is our model and our guide, and our transformation is wrought through Him, but this does not preclude a natural readiness or base. Indeed it presupposes it, for grace builds on nature, and it is man himself who is uplifted and restored.[7] For Erasmus, then, there is no opposition or conflict between the doctrine of Christ and the aspirations and potential of mankind, and this perhaps is the most basic reason why he can be called a Christian humanist.

Describing these features of Erasmus' thought serves not only to introduce him in this essay, but to lay the groundwork for a discussion of his views on war and peace. There is a remarkable unity and coherence in all his work, but the mark of his Christian humanism is seen nowhere more clearly than in his attitude and writings on the subject of peace. We shall turn now to this latter theme.

A clear and simple fact stands out. Erasmus was a pacifist; one might even say he was the first pacifist to declare himself so unequivocally and express himself so fully on the question. The definition of pacifism in the Webster's International Dictionary admirably describes his point of view: "Opposition to war or to the use of military force for any purpose; especially an attitude of mind opposing all war, emphasizing the defects of military training and the cost of war, and advocating settlement of international disputes entirely by arbitration." We need not enter into a niggling discussion as to whether his pacifism was total and absolute or not. He did perhaps feel that in the last resort a defensive war against the invading Turks was permissible, but the whole bent of his mind, his ideal, his constant plea was peace.[8] He believed war was a madness and a folly; he saw it as a disastrous, corrupting, and ruinous affair; he condemned it as the very antithesis of the doctrine of Christ. This last conviction is especially prominent in the attitude he expressed; it is his bedrock argument, his most insistent and characteristic line of attack, and the theme that Christianity means peace is one he continually reiterates. "What else is our religion than peace in the Holy Spirit?"[9] "The sum and substance of our religion is peace and concord."[10] "God is the author not of dissension but of peace."[11]

The pacifism of Erasmus, however, is far more than a pious revulsion at war or a broad religious aspiration for peace. Scholars are just now beginning to discover its foundation and true meaning. It is rooted in his theology, and it is an essential part, a very fundamental part, of his understanding of the nature of Christianity and the Church. Several studies have recently called attention to the deeper dimension of Erasmus' concern for peace.[12] Our purpose, however, is not so much to probe its theological roots as to examine the more explicit character of his pacifism. To do this we shall look at the two essays where he gives the fullest and most comprehensive statement of his views on the subject of war and peace—an essay in the *Adages* entitled *Dulce bellum inexpertis* and a little book entitled *Querela pacis* or *The Complaint of Peace*.[13] He expressed himself in many other places, of course, on this subject, but the two writings singled out are unquestionably his most important pacifist declarations.[14]

Dulce bellum inexpertis—the title is an ancient proverb meaning "war is sweet to those who have not tried it"—was first published in the revised and enlarged edition of the *Adages*, called *Proverbiorum chiliades*, which Johann Froben brought out in Basel in 1515. This edition, inaugurating the most significant phase of Erasmus' career, is one of the humanist's major works, and the essay *Dulce bellum inexpertis* is the longest and most notable essay in the volume.[15] The *Bellum*, to use a short title, was printed separately by Froben in 1517, and it saw many subsequent publications. Its actual composition occurred most probably prior to 1515, and it was composed in the context of a Europe plunged in war. These latter circumstances explain the appearance of the essay and require a brief comment.

Pope Julius II, reigning from 1503 to 1513, had defeated the Venetians with the aid of France and now turned against France and sought to oust her from her occupation in northern Italy. To accomplish this he formed a league with Ferdinand of Spain in 1511 and with his former enemy the Venetians. In 1513 England joined the papal side. Widespread war now flared, and nearly all the European states were drawn into the fray. "That trumpet of Julius had summoned the whole world to war," wrote Erasmus in a letter to Cardinal Raffaelle Riario in May 1515.[16] The French were driven from the Duchy of Milan, the Spanish took Navarre, the English attacked France on the continent, the Scots invaded England. Julius died in early 1513 and was succeeded by the Medici Pope Leo X, but the events he had precipitated by his league against France in 1511 (and which France had in turn precipitated by her earlier invasion of Italy) continued to run their destructive course when Erasmus wrote and published the *Bellum*. He himself had been personally involved in these events and had been deeply affected by them. He had seen Julius in action in Italy, having witnessed his triumphal entry into Bologna in November 1506; he had observed something of the shock and devastation of war; he had beheld England to which he returned from Italy in 1509 with high expectation gradually drawn into the conflict; he had suffered the loss of a noble friend, the son of the king of Scotland whom he once had tutored, cut down in the flower of his youth in the battle of Flodden Field in October 1513. Every hope or possibility of a better world seemed shattered by this madness which held Christendom in its grip. If "it was Julius II who turned Erasmus into a pacifist," as it has been said, it was certainly the continuation of the struggle and its ruinous effects that account for the great protest he launched in the *Bellum*.[17] In this sense the essay was a necessary prologue to the work of renewal and reform he was so anxious to achieve.

The *Bellum* can be divided into two fairly equal parts. In the first half Erasmus begins by contrasting the image of man as nature meant him to be with the brutal and monstrous picture of war. He then gives a rather interesting account of how the evil of war arose in the first place, and he concludes with a brief comparison between the joys of peaceful times and the dire effects of war. In the second half of the essay Erasmus raises the question of Christians' waging war, especially against one another, in view of the example and teaching of Christ, and he explores this issue quite thoroughly, not avoiding a discussion of the thorny problem of war against the Turks. This second and slightly larger half is remarkable for its presentation and defense of the Gospel ideal of love and non-violence, of unity and peace.

This two-fold division of the *Bellum* reflects, it seems clear, that feature of Erasmus' Christian humanism we have noted: namely, that he saw Christianity as in accord with human nature, as completing and crowning all that is best in creation. Thus war is not only proscribed for the Christian who must follow Christ's commandment of love, but it is unworthy of man as man and alien to his nature. It is the latter point that Erasmus discusses in the first half of the essay. That man was made for peace and friendship and mutual aid he deduces from man's physical characteristics and appearance, from his possession of the faculties of speech and reason, from his innate desire for companionship, from his love of learning. In addition, he states that nature distributes her endowments among men so that each must look to another for what is needful or useful and each may take a delight in being of service to all. War violates this natural disposition and interdependence and indeed brings a host of evils in its wake, including further and more general war, for "war is born from war." These considerations lead Erasmus to think that war is the product of hell, the work of Furies. Nature herself will exclaim as she views man the warrior: "I see nothing left in him of the man I made. What evil genius has spoilt my work?"[18] Erasmus pursues this theme of the origin of the evil of war and gives a curious and ingenious explanation. Primitive man, he tells us, sometimes had to fight wild beasts. Surviving these onslaughts men began to hunt animals and wear their skins and eat their carcasses, and they proceeded from the harmful beasts to the harmless ones. Having thus gained practice in killing, "men were incited by anger to turn their attacks on men," knowing that "man too could be killed with very little trouble."[19] At first it was single combat, but then groups banded together for the fray, and more sophisticated arms were invented, and the battle became more ferocious. War had come into being. "And so little by little, military science developed with civilization, and city began to declare war on city, region on region, kingdom on kingdom."[20] Although some rules and restraints were still observed, later these disappeared when the struggle for empire intensified and the worst rogues came to power. From these beginnings, Erasmus concludes, we have reached "the point of lunacy" that we see today. "We are continually at war," and worst of all Christians make war, even against other Christians. Moreover, we applaud it, we justify it, "we drag Christ into it."[21] Whether scientific or not, Erasmus' account of the evolution of war has considerable dramatic value and force, and viewing man as pacifist by nature he had to give some explanation of war's development and present-day intensity.

What follows next is a brief description of the benefits and joys of peace as compared with the destruction and misfortunes of war—a comparison whose details recall the frescoes on Good and Bad Government by Ambrogio Lorenzetti in the Palazzo Pubblico in Siena.[22] Erasmus then advances to the theme of the second half of his essay: the antithesis between war and the doctrine of Christ. Acknowledging that pagans succumbed to the madness of war he now seeks to understand how Christians could do likewise, Christians "who are of the household of one Church, who are members of the same body and glory in the same Head, that is Christ."[23] What could be more opposed than war to Christ's commandment of love or to His prayer to the Father that "they may all be one"? "Examine the whole of His teaching," Erasmus demands; "you will find nothing anywhere which does not breathe the spirit of peace, which does not savor of love."[24]

In this second part of the *Bellum* Erasmus is speaking with particular relevance to the Europe of his day—to the Europe that called itself Christian but whose nations were locked in bloody combat and whose Pope had led the way. How has this come about, "this plague that creeps through the people of Christ"?[25] He claims that the influence of Aristotle has corrupted theology and that the acceptance of certain principles of Roman law has distorted the Gospel. False standards and false values have gained such a hold that Christians now are worse than pagans and make war with less humanity and restraint. "We pseudo-Christians," his voice begins to rise, "we only copy the worst of the ancient world—or rather we outdo it."[26] To the objection that God allowed the Jews to make war he replies that Christ ordered us to put up the sword; to the objections of a "just war" or a war of defense he points to Christ's injunctions telling us to repay evil with good; to the argument that popes have made war or that certain of the Fathers have approved it he stresses the higher authority of Christ Himself; to the excuse that a right or a just claim is at stake he emphasizes the lack of proportion between these often paltry claims and the cost and destruction of war. In the latter situation he advises compromise and arbitration. "The world has so many earnest and learned bishops, so many venerable abbots, so many aged peers with the wisdom of long experience, so many councils, so many conclaves. Why do we not use their arbitration to settle these childish disputes between princes?"[27] By the same token Erasmus believed that the chief prelates of the Church had the obligation to act as peacemakers when quarrels arose among the princes.[28]

Finally he opposes even war against the Turks, the old enemy of the Christian faith and at this time a long-standing threat to Christian Europe.

> To me [he writes] it does not even seem recommendable that we should now be preparing war against the Turks. The Christian religion is in a bad way, if its safety depends on this sort of defense. Nor is it consistent to make good Christians under these auspices. What is taken by the sword is lost by the sword. Are you anxious to win the Turks for Christ? Let us not display our wealth, our armies, our strength. Let them see in us not only the name, but the unmistakable marks of a Christian: a blameless life, the wish to do good even to our enemies, a tolerance which will withstand all injuries, contempt of money, heedlessness of glory, life held lightly; let them hear that heavenly doctrine which is in accordance with this kind of life. These are the best arms with which to defeat the Turks.[29]

Erasmus expanded this portion of his essay considerably several years later when the Turkish danger was even more acute, but his theme remained the same: the best way to fight the Turks and win them for Christ is to be Christian ourselves and show them conduct worthy of the Gospel.[30]

In the concluding pages Erasmus states his view that war in Christian Europe proceeds either from stupidity or from wickedness. He particularly castigates princes who resort to war as "a way of confirming their tyranny over their subjects," and he stresses again the cost and dire consequences of war. In a final exhortation he calls upon the Christian powers to embrace the cause of peace. "Calamity itself leads us to this; Christ beckons us to it."[31] It is his hope that the princes will respond to the call to peace of the Medici Pope then reigning, Leo X, who will garner greater glory from a return to peace than his predecessor Julius ever won from his many wars.

In any study of Erasmus' pacifism the *Bellum* deserves major emphasis because it is a comprehensive statement and the most impassioned plea for peace of the great humanist. It can also be seen as opening a significant phase—a climactic phase—in his career as a reformer and as playing a fundamental role in his reform program. The revival, the Christian renewal, he hoped would come could hardly be conceived in a Europe torn by war. "Peace," he declares, "is the mother and nurse of all that is good."[32] It is both the prerequisite and the great blessing of a better day. It is interesting to note too that the *Bellum* together with its companion essays in the *Adages* appeared the year prior to Thomas More's *Utopia*, whose publication Erasmus arranged for at Louvain in late 1516, and that there is a concordance of purpose and theme between these two works. The figure of Raphael Hythloday, the narrator in *Utopia* and More's partner in the dialogue, bears a resemblance to Erasmus in many of the views he expresses. His reluctance to enter the service of a prince and compromise thereby his lofty ideals suggests Erasmus' desire for independence and freedom. His attitude toward war also corresponds with Erasmus'. If he was in the privy council of the king of France, Hythloday would tell the king to stop his war in Italy and stay home and govern France well, for war is disastrous and a prince's first duty is to see to the welfare and happiness of his own people.[33] Not only is this attitude echoed in the *Bellum*, but it is the precise theme of another and shorter essay Erasmus also published in the *Adages* in 1515. This essay is entitled *Spartam nactus es, hanc orna*, the title being a Latin proverb which literally means "You have obtained Sparta, adorn it," but which can be freely rendered as "Take care of those obligations you have."[34] It can be read as an appendage of the *Bellum*, developing at some length the specific point in the case against war which Hythloday also made in *Utopia*.

The other key statement by Erasmus on the subject of war and peace, the little book *Querela pacis* or *The Complaint of Peace*, appeared in December 1517, more than two years after the *Bellum*. It also was first published by Johann Froben in Basel, and there were many subsequent editions, including an English translation in 1559. It is about the same length as the *Bellum* but more formal in tone, its framework being an address or sermon delivered by Peace, who is personified. It was written in the same context of international turmoil as the *Bellum*, but its immediate purpose and occasion were more specific. Erasmus composed it in the latter part of 1516 at the request of Jean le Sauvage, Chancellor of Burgundy and a leading figure in the court of the young Prince Charles of the Netherlands. The circumstances in back of this request are most interesting.[35]

In 1516 Jean le Sauvage and Guillaume de Croy, Lord of Chièvres, were the chief councilors of Prince Charles who had also become King of Spain in January that year (and was destined in 1519 to become the Holy Roman Emperor Charles V).[36] They had recently secured his independence from the tutelage of his aunt Margaret of Austria who had served as his regent in the Low Countries, and they were now pressing a "national policy," as Pirenne calls it, in opposition to the anti-French orientation inspired by Hapsburg dynastc interests and supported by Margaret of Austria. This new policy aimed at restoring peace and establishing close ties with France, and it sought to convene the European princes in a conference at Cambrai to work out a general peace settlement. Erasmus, in short, was enlisted by le Sauvage and Chièvres to help to further this policy.

When he was asked to write this essay on peace, Erasmus was at the height of his renown. Europe's most famous scholar, he was also a native as well as a frequent visitor to the Low Countries during these years, and he himself had been made a councilor to Prince Charles in 1515.[37] The post was an honorary rather than a strictly functional one, but it was in his capacity as a councilor in the court of Charles that he originally composed *The Complaint of Peace*. Nor was this the only treatise he composed in that capacity. He previously wrote and dedicated to Charles his *Institutio principis christiani*, a moralistic treatise on the education of a Christian prince.[38] Much broader in scope than *The Complaint of Peace*, it contains nevertheless, as we might expect, in its final chapter an incisive condemnation of war and an exhortation to peace. The *Complaint*, however, is a far more developed and detailed pacifist statement.

As mentioned above, it is in the form of an address given by the personification of Peace. She complains that men disdain and reject her, and she bewails not simply her own injury but the misery and calamity that befall men as a result. The structure of the argument is very similar to that in the *Bellum*: war is first viewed as contrary to man's nature, it is then seen as alien to the teaching of Christ. The development of this latter part of the argument in the *Complaint* is particularly impressive.[39] It begins with the prophecy of Isaiah that the Messiah will come as the Prince of Peace, it reviews the many scriptural injunctions and episodes wherein Christ taught that men must live in concord and mutual love, and it closes with an evocation of the unity of Christians in the Church and in their hope of the heavenly Jerusalem. But alas, laments Peace, what contradiction there is! Men "break and cut off all the bands of nature and of Christ," they war without cease.[40] This leads to a discussion of the causes of war in present-day Europe: ambition, cupidity, anger, the evil counsel of priests and bishops and even popes. Erasmus again takes the opportunity to castigate Julius II and other prelates and friars who blew their trumpets and called the nations to war. As men obeyed Julius when he summoned them to war, he asks—or rather Peace asks—why do they not obey Leo who exhorts them to peace?

A lecture then follows on the duties of a prince.[41] He must serve not his own profit but the commonweal; he must remember that he rules men who are free and Christian; he must not do those things which endanger peace; he must labor to adorn his own kingdom and make it flourish. Again the advice given is remarkably like the counsel which Raphael Hythloday in *Utopia* would proffer the king of France, but in this instance Erasmus is actually offering it to the young Charles of the Netherlands, King of Spain. We have a bond here not simply between Erasmus and More but also between the aims and ideals of the humanists and the politics—the power politics—of their time. As Garrett Mattingly has warned in his *Renaissance Diplomacy*, we should not assume that the two were totally and inexorably at odds.[42]

In the final pages of the *Complaint* Erasmus continues to probe the occasions of war and to lift men's sights above their contentions and divisions. "This world is the common country of all men," he declares, just as the Church is the common family of all, and these bonds must reconcile us.[43] The dire consequences of war should lead us to avoid it, and princes especially must realize war's evil effects—its waste, its expense, its disorder, its corrupting influence, the unholy spectacle as well as opportunity it affords the Turks. After the miseries of war too long borne, Peace concludes her lament: let us grow wise. United by nature as well as by Christ let us seek peace.

Such then is the message of Erasmus on the subject of war and peace.

His pacifism is rooted deeply in his Christian consciousness and is an essential aspect of his Christian humanism. He condemned war as destructive of the well-being and potential of mankind, he saw it as a violation of all that Christ represented and taught. His opposition to war was also an important and integral part of his reform program, that is, of his life's work. In a résumé of his goals and activities which he addressed to a critic in 1527 he assigned it first place, and he wrote: "I have vigorously raised my voice against the wars which for so many years now we see agitating nearly all of Christendom."[44] In fact, he launched a crusade against the mindless slaughter he saw going on in the Europe of his time. He sought especially to influence the powerful, those who make the decisions regarding war and peace, and *The Complaint of Peace* is a major example of this effort.[45] Erasmus' pacifism thus was not the dream of a scholar in an ivory tower. It was conceived and developed as highly relevant advice, and it was advanced as practical counsel and instruction for the Christian rulers as well as for other important contemporaries of his day. He was hopeful too, especially in 1516–17 with a new and more promising group of princes at the helm, that Europe would have peace and that a better day would dawn.[46]

But wars did not cease; Christendom and its princes did not respond to his call for peace. In fact, divisions, antagonism, and warfare increased and intensified in the years ahead. How meaningful then was Erasmus' pacifism, how effective his effort or valid his advice? Two scholars have recently given a critical appraisal on this score.[47] Both have seen the message of Erasmus as politically inadequate and unrealistic. One of the critiques hails Erasmus as "a voice crying in the wilderness," but withal it finds him naïve and overly optimistic about human nature. From a certain viewpoint these strictures can be made, but one must remember that Erasmus is writing not as a modern political scientist aware of "the dynamics of power" (whatever the term may mean) but as a Christian moralist and reformer well aware of the follies and crimes which men are guilty of. His aim was not to describe, in the fashion of Machiavelli, the political maneuvers or the diplomatic evasions of his day but to induce men, particularly those in positions of influence or power, to act in a more responsible and Christian way. In brief, he was exhorting men to peace; he was not merely observing and analyzing the international scene.

He must be judged chiefly on this basis—that is, on the intrinsic worth of his exhortation. Was his aim valid, were his arguments cogent, was his appeal substantial and well made? To turn pragmatist and seek to evaluate his message by its apparent political results or by the events that followed its circulation in the Europe of his time is the wrong approach. That wars continued is quite another question. There are any number of reasons for that, the least of them being the inadequacy of Erasmus' thought and action in this cause. Honesty is still a virtue though there is a great deal of dishonesty and corruption in our human relationships. So too the moral obligation to live in peace, respectful of the rights of others, still binds though there are breakdowns and violations too numerous to record. Erasmus' pacifism must be seen in terms of a moral principle and a human ideal and not in terms of a politically effective doctrine for its day or a cure for the scourge of war. Men do evil deeds despite the good counsel they receive or the arguments and encouragement given to follow a better course.

Is there meaning or purpose, then, in Erasmus' plea for peace? One must reply, of course, that there is. It simply should not be judged in terms of its immediate effectiveness in ending war. There would be very few ideals or moral principles left if we approached them all in so pragmatic a fashion. History is not the story of the triumph of morality but a drama of conflict between man's hopes and his imperfections, between what should be (or what men believe should be) and the difficulties and obstacles inherent in our earthbound existence. We cannot, however, preoccupy ourselves only with the latter. The former also play a part. They give direction, they supply motive force, they enable men to make what progress men do make. If man's nobler aims and ideals rarely effect an immediate transformation in the world at large, they can and do effect gradual change and, more importantly perhaps, personal growth and transformation. "It is too much even to hope that all men will be good," Erasmus wrote in *The Education of a Christian Prince*,[48] but one can hope that some men will and that they will have influence. There is really no alternative for such an attitude of hopefulness, if the pessimism or cynicism that oftentimes overtakes the observer of the historical scene is to be surmounted.

Rabelais closed the strange prophecy referred to at the beginning of this essay with the words:

> How praiseworthy he
> Who shall have persevered even to the end!

This can also be applied to Erasmus. Discouragement and defeat were his personal lot, but he remained remarkably constant in his convictions and his principles to the last. Though the world was sundered the religious faith that underlay his pacifism held firm.

NOTES

1. Rabelais, *The Histories of Gargantua and Pantagruel*, trans. J. M. Cohen (Baltimore, 1955), p. 162. On the enigmatic prophecy see M. A. Screech, "The Sense of the *Enigme en prophétie*," *Bibliothèque d'Humanisme et Renaissance*, 18 (1956), 392–404.

2. On Erasmus and Rabelais see Lucien Febvre, *Le problème de l'incroyance au XVIe siècle. La religion de Rabelais* (Paris, 1968), pp. 281–306. In a letter to Erasmus in November 1532 Rabelais declared his indebtedness to him (Allen, X, 130).

3. Werner Jaeger, *Early Christianity and Greek Paideia* (Oxford, 1969), p. 101; Etienne Gilson, *The Spirit of Medieval Philosophy*, trans. A. H. C. Downes (New York, 1940), Chap. VI: "Christian Optimism"; *idem*, "L'humanisme médiéval et la Renaissance" in *Les idées et les lettres* (Paris, 1932), pp. 171–96; and Augustin Renaudet, *Humanisme et Renaissance* (Geneva, 1958), Chap. IV: "Autour d'une définition de l'humanisme," esp. pp. 39–53.

4. *The Enchiridion of Erasmus*, trans. Raymond Himelick (Bloomington, 1963), p. 56, and Gilson, *The Spirit of Medieval Philosophy*, pp. 27–28. St. Augustine's declaration is in his *De doctrina christiana*, Bk. II, Chap. XVIII. St. Thomas' statement is in the *Summa theologica*, Ia IIae, Q. 109, art. 1, ad 1.

5. *The Colloquies of Erasmus*, trans. Craig R. Thompson (Chicago, 1965), pp. 65–68. This particular colloquy called *Convivium religiosum* or *The Godly Feast* is one of Erasmus' greatest.

6. CHR, p. 100. The same thought is expressed in Erasmus' annotation on Matt. 11:30 in his *Annotationes in Novum Testamentum*.

7. Jean-Claude Margolin, *Recherches érasmiennes* (Geneva, 1969), pp. 31–41. Erasmus' attitude corresponds with the dictum of St. Thomas: "Grace does not destroy nature but completes it." *Summa theologica*, I, Q. 1, art. 8, ad 2, and also I, Q. 2, art. 2, ad 1.

8. José A. Fernandez, "Erasmus on the Just War," *Journal of the History of Ideas*, 34 (April–June 1973), 209–26.

9. Letter to Jodocus Jonas, May 10, 1521 (CHR, p. 151).

10. Preface to his edition of St. Hilary, January 1523, in Allen, V, 177; see Appendix, below.

11. Preface to his edition of St. Irenaeus, August 1526, in Allen, VI, 384.

12. See in particular Georges Chantraine, "*Mysterium* et *Sacramentum* dans le '*Dulce Bellum*'," in *Colloquium erasmianum* (Mons, 1968), pp. 33–45; James K. McConica, "Erasmus and the Grammar of Consent," in *Scrinium erasmianum* (2 vols.; Leiden, 1969), II, 96–99; and Jean-Pierre Massaut, "Humanisme et spiritualité chez Erasme," *Dictionnaire de spiritualité*, fasc. 46–47, col. 1016.

13. *Dulce bellum inexpertis* in English translation is in Margaret Mann Phillips, *The 'Adages' of Erasmus* (Cambridge, 1964), pp. 308–53. Our references to it will be to this text. There is a modern Latin–French edition by Yvonne Remy and René Dunil-Marquebreucq (Brussels, 1953). *Querela pacis* in an early English translation—that of Thomas Paynell of 1559—is in Erasmus, *The Complaint of Peace*, ed. W. J. Hirten (New York, 1946). Our references to it will be to this edition. The Latin text and an excellent introduction can be found in Elise Constantinescue Bagdat, *La "Querela Pacis" d'Erasme* (Paris, 1924).

14. A comprehensive anthology of Erasmus' writings on this subject, well annotated, is Erasme, *Guerre et paix dans la pensée d'Erasme*, ed. Jean-Claude Margolin (Paris, 1973). See also Robert P. Adams, *The Better Part of Valor* (Seattle, 1962) for a general survey and analysis of Erasmus' writings in this field as well as those of More, Colet and Vives.

15. Mrs. Phillips has an excellent discussion of this edition in *The 'Adages' of Erasmus*, pp. 96–121. She calls it "the Utopian edition" and compares many of its themes with those in Thomas More's *Utopia* which was first published in 1516. The edition also began Erasmus' friendship and collaboration with the famous Basel printer, Johann Froben.

16. Allen, II, 70.

17. The quotation is Mrs. Phillips' in *The 'Adages' of Erasmus*, p. 105. Erasmus' aversion to Julius II is well known. He was most likely the author of the anonymous satire on Julius' war-making entitled *Julius exclusus*, and certainly the image of the wicked pope "shedding Christian blood" in *The Praise of Folly*, composed in England in 1509 shortly after he returned from Italy, is Julius. The *Bellum*, however, was written after Julius' death and the election of Leo X in March 1513 (the latter is referred to in the essay). In fact it seems to have a concise prototype in a letter Erasmus wrote to Antony of Bergen, abbot at St. Omer, in March 1514. Allen I, 551–54.

18. *The 'Adages' of Erasmus*, p. 316. Erasmus' "anthropology" finds at least partial confirmation in a recent scientific work on man's origins and evolution: Richard E. Leakey and Roger Lewin, *Origins* (New York, 1977). The authors reject the view that early man was belligerent by nature, and they stress that social cooperation was a key factor in human evolution.

19. *The 'Adages' of Erasmus*, p. 319.

20. *Ibid.*, pp. 319–20.

21. *Ibid.*, p. 322.

22. *Ibid.*, pp. 323–24. Erasmus was in Siena in early 1509 with the young son of James IV of Scotland who was later killed at Flodden Field. It is quite likely he saw the Lorenzetti frescoes in the great Sala della Pace.

23. *Ibid.*, p. 327.

24. *Ibid.*, p. 328.

25. *Ibid.*, p. 330.

26. *Ibid.*, pp. 333, 335.

27. *Ibid.*, p. 343.

28. In his letter to Antony of Bergen in March 1514 Erasmus wrote: "It is the special duty of the Roman Pontiff, of the cardinals, of the bishops, of the abbots to settle the disagreements of the Christian princes" (Allen, I, 553).

29. *The 'Adages' of Erasmus*, p. 344. Erasmus' attitude also calls to mind the original intention of St. Ignatius Loyola and his early companions. Their chief desire was to go to Jerusalem "to spend their lives in the service of souls." *The Autobiography of St. Ignatius Loyola*, trans. Joseph F. O'Callaghan, ed. John C. Olin (New York, 1974), p. 80.

30. Erasmus frequently expressed himself in this vein about war with the Turks. Another notable example is in the Letter to Paul Volz which served as the preface to his 1518 edition of the *Enchiridion militis christiani* (CHR, pp. 112–15). On this subject see also Fernandez, "Erasmus on the Just War," 218–20.

31. *The 'Adages' of Erasmus*, p. 352.

32. *Ibid.*, p. 323.

33. St. Thomas More, *Utopia*, ed. Edward Surtz, s.j. (New Haven, 1964), pp. 40–48.

34. *The 'Adages' of Erasmus*, pp. 300–8.

35. Allen, I, 18–19, and III, 13–15. See also Bagdat, La *"Querela Pacis,"* Chap. I; Margolin's introduction to *Querela pacis* in *Guerre et paix*, pp. 197–203; and Henri Pirenne, *Histoire de Belgique*, 3 (Brussels, 1907), 77–81, 159, et passim.

36. Born at Ghent in 1500, Charles was the heir of the Dukes of Burgundy who ruled the many provinces that the Netherlands comprised. His parents were Philip of Burgundy (d. 1506) and the Infanta Joanna of Spain. His maternal grandfather was Ferdinand of Spain (d. 1516), his paternal grandfather was the Hapsburg Emperor Maximilian (d. 1519). Charles succeeded to the titles of all his forebears.

37. Through the efforts of Jean le Sauvage, as Erasmus tells us in his *Compendium vitae* (CHR, p. 28). Allen, I, 51. See also Allen, II, 161, n. 18.

38. Erasmus, *The Education of a Christian Prince*, ed. and trans. Lester K. Born (New York, 1936). The work was first published by Froben in June 1516.

39. *The Complaint of Peace*, pp. 17–28.

40. *Ibid.*, p. 29.

41. *Ibid.*, pp. 40–44.

42. Mattingly, *Renaissance Diplomacy* (Boston, 1955), pp. 166–67.

43. *The Complaint of Peace*, pp. 47–48.

44. Allen, VII, 208.

45. Another major example is his letter to Francis I of France of December 1, 1523, which served as the dedicatory preface to his Paraphrase on the Gospel of St. Mark. It is a forthright plea for peace to a king actively engaged in war. He had previously dedicated his Paraphrases on the other three Gospels to Prince Charles, to the latter's brother Ferdinand, and to Henry VIII of England, with the hope, as he told Francis I, "that the evangelical spirit might join together your hearts as harmoniously as the evangelical text unites your names." Allen, V, 352–61, and *Guerre et Paix*, pp. 15–16 and 266–82.

46. This hopefulness finds memorable expression in a letter to Wolfgang Capito of February 26, 1517. With peace being restored in Christendom, Erasmus saw that "a golden age would arise very soon." Allen, II, 487–92.

47. Fernandez, "Erasmus on the Just War," and Pierre Brachin, "Vox clamantis in Deserto, Réflexions sur le pacifisme d'Erasme," *Colloquia Erasmiana Turonensia*, ed. Jean-Claude Margolin (2 vols.; Toronto, 1972), I, 247–75.

48. P. 143. More wrote in *Utopia* (Surtz ed., p. 50): "What you cannot turn to good you must make as little bad as you can. For it is impossible that all should be well unless all men were good, a situation which I do not expect for a great many years to come!"

3

ERASMUS AND THE CHURCH FATHERS

> I have tried to call back theology, sunk too far in
> sophistical subtleties, to the sources and to ancient
> simplicity.
>
> ERASMUS to JEAN GACHI, October 1527

THE CHIEF AIM OF ERASMUS in his life's work as a humanist scholar was to restore theology. In his times this meant to replace the theology then being taught and practiced as a professional science by a more adequate study of Holy Scripture and the Fathers of the early Church. The goal involved the rejection of late medieval scholasticism and vigorous criticism of "modern" theologians, particularly Occamists and Scotists, and it embraced above all a return to the sources—to the ancient and genuine theology, *vetus ac vera theologia*, of the first Christian centuries. As a purpose and perspective this aim was highly characteristic of the era we call the Renaissance, and as an intellectual ideal it motivated one of the most dynamic movements associated with "the revival of learning." In this instance the revival was explicitly a reform and religious renewal, and it may even be said to imply the notion of rebirth in the spiritual sense of the word.[1]

Nearly the whole corpus of Erasmus' writings and work, from his first letter to Colet in 1499 to his posthumous edition of Origen in 1536, can be drawn on to illustrate these remarks, but an accolade rendered him by a young scholar–priest in 1522 at the peak of his career serves as well as any other text to clarify and heighten the main point we are making.[2] Urban Rieger, recently cathedral preacher at Augsburg, wrote Erasmus to praise and thank him for his scholarly endeavors in the field of theology. He hailed Erasmus as "the prince of theologians" and "the first author in our times of the rebirth of theology" and listed his achievements, declaring that he "called back theologians from the very turbid waters of the scholastics to the source of sacred letters" and urged them to go to "the ancient theologians"—to "the clearest source." He ended his letter with a climactic tribute and urgent appeal:

The substance of this essay was delivered as a lecture at the Sixteenth Century Studies Conference held at The University of Iowa in October 1975.

Thus you have summoned as with a trumpet the entire world to the philosophy of Christ. We do not doubt that you were born to restore theology. Therefore fulfill your destiny and purge with your most learned hand Augustine and Hilary that we may distinguish the spurious from the genuine, as in previous years you did most successfully with Jerome.

This stress on going back to the ancient theologians, that is, to the Fathers of the early Church, and on their vast superiority over the "modern" ones, that is, the late medieval schoolmen, is a constant theme in Erasmus. It explains in the first place why he undertook the enormous task of editing and publishing so many of the early Fathers. In a preface in the great edition of St. Jerome which appeared in 1516 Erasmus wrote:

We have undertaken this labor neither for the glory nor for the gain but only to serve by our industry the candidates of that ancient theology which I would judge alone to be theology if I did not fear so many hostile bands of critics. At least let me not hesitate to proclaim that this theology is far more conducive to Christian learning and a pious life than that which is now treated far and wide in the schools, crammed so full with Aristotelian principles, contaminated by such sophistical nonsense, not to say dreams, entangled so in the labyrinths of vain and petty questions that, if Jerome himself came back to life or Paul, he would find nothing there resembling theology.[3]

Not surprisingly, one of the most striking passages exalting the early Fathers is in Erasmus' key treatise on theological study, the *Ratio verae theologiae* of 1518, where in several places he urges students to read the old commentators and writers rather than the scholastics. If anyone wants to know why, he argues,

let him compare those ancient theologians—Origen, Basil, Chrysostom, Jerome—with these modern ones. There he will see a golden river flowing, here some shallow rivulets which are neither very pure nor faithful to their source. There the oracles of eternal truth thunder forth, here you hear the little inventions of men which vanish like dreams the more closely you examine them. There an edifice rises on high supported on the solid foundations of Scripture, here a hollow and monstrous scaffold built on the worthless quibbles of men or even on low flattery rises to an enormous height. There you will be completely delighted and satisfied as in the most fruitful gardens, here you will be lacerated and tormented among barren thornbushes. There everything is full of grandeur, here nothing is splendid but is for the most part unclean and little in keeping with the dignity of theology.[4]

In Erasmus' program to restore theology, Holy Scripture, of course, came first, especially the Gospels and Epistles where the teachings of Christ are to be found in all their original purity and splendor. Here was the well from which every Christian must draw before all else, and the reform of theology as well as the revitalization of Christian morality and life depended primarily on a return to Scripture. "Is he a theologian, let alone a Christian," Erasmus asks in the introduction to his New Testament, "who has not read the literature of Christ?"[5] But after this literature came the Fathers. Their authority derived from their closeness in time as well as in spirit to the divine source, and their chief value lay in interpreting and helping us to understand the sacred text. Moreover they instructed and inspired us in living a Christian life, for theology was essentially practical in Erasmus' view—a guide to life rather than a subject for debate, a matter of our transformation rather than of speculation. In terms of a more authentic and effective transmission of the doctrine of Christ the early Fathers by far excelled, and it was for this reason that Erasmus cherished them and sought to make them better known.

The work he undertook to accomplish this was truly enormous—herculean, to use his own term—and to it he devoted, as Henri de Lubac has pointed out, "the better part of his existence."[6] Yet strangely enough historians and biographers have not paid it the close attention it deserves. All have not been as oblivious or neglectful as Preserved Smith, who in his life of Erasmus dismissed the great mass of his patristic work and scholarship and the role it played in his thought and reform efforts in a few pages in a chapter on Erasmus' "miscellaneous writings," but it has rarely been treated with the detail or the emphasis it requires.[7] I do not propose to do justice to the subject in this short essay. I want simply to sketch the outline and indicate the scope and importance of this major segment of his life's work.

The first of Erasmus' patristic editions was the nine-volume *Opera* of St. Jerome. It was published in the late summer of 1516 by Johann Froben of Basel, and it is the most famous and perhaps the most important of the many editions of the Fathers Erasmus will produce. As a scholar and saint Jerome had long been Erasmus' favorite. When he was a young monk at Steyn he had known and treasured the letters of Jerome, and he set about the task of restoring their text and writing a commentary on them at the very outset of his scholarly career.[8] We can truly view this undertaking as the first stage in his project to renew theology—a project which John Colet had inspired and one which by 1500 had begun earnestly to engage him.[9] Other tasks and enterprises, however, took precedence over editing St. Jerome, although Erasmus continued to work on him, and indeed lectured on his writings when he taught at Cambridge in 1511–1513. Even as late as 1512 he was not ready to take up the offer of the Paris printer Josse Badius Ascensius to publish a new edition of the saint's letters, and a few years later when he was prepared to go to press with such a work it was with Froben in Basel rather than with Badius that he made contact.

Erasmus first came to Basel and began his long association with Johann Froben in August 1514. He was now reaching the height of his renown, and during the next few years he will publish some of his most important work. His reform criticism and aims will also become more focused and more intense. 1516, in fact, is an *annus mirabilis* in the story of Erasmian humanism. It is the year of his Greek and Latin New Testament as well as of the St. Jerome; it is the year of his *Education of a Christian Prince* and of his *Querela pacis*; it is the year, too, of Thomas More's *Utopia* whose first publication Erasmus arranged at Louvain. The Jerome edition was a major factor in his coming to Basel in the first place. He had learned that the Amerbach–Froben press was preparing a new edition of St. Jerome, and, impressed by a publication of his *Adagia* which they brought out in 1513 and by the resources of the firm (they acquired an extensive Greek font in 1514), he betook himself to the busy city on the Rhine in the summer of 1514. "The decision brought together the greatest scholar and the greatest printer in Transalpine Europe," in the words of P. S. Allen.[10]

Johann Amerbach had died the preceding December, and it was his partner Froben who now greeted Erasmus. It had been Amerbach's ambition, however, to publish good texts of the four great Doctors of the western Church, and having brought out an edition of St. Ambrose in 1492 and of St. Augustine in 1506 he had begun preparation of an edition of St. Jerome. Considerable effort had already gone into the correcting and restoring of Jerome's text, to which Conrad Pellican, Johann Reuchlin, the learned Dominican Johann Kuno, the Carthusian prior at Freiburg Gregory Reisch, as well as the scholarly sons of Amerbach, Bruno, Basil, and Boniface, had all contributed.[11] Erasmus now joined this project, devoting himself primarily to the letters on which he had long been working, but assisting in the completion of the entire edition. He has given us several vivid accounts of the problems involved in "reviving" St. Jerome, declaring that "it cost Jerome less to write his books than us to restore them."[12] The arduous task of collating and correcting, restoring and annotating, however, at last was finished, the manuscript went to press, and by September 1516 the nine folio volumes of the great edition were on the market.

Erasmus' share was chiefly the letters of St. Jerome, and these are contained in the first four volumes. The other five are scriptural commentaries for the most part and include a trilingual psalter. The term "letters" in this instance covers a wide variety of instructional and polemical writing which constitutes the most important segment of the Jerome corpus. Their editing was the most difficult task of all, for though there were many earlier editions of the letters the spurious and falsely ascribed were mixed with the genuine, and there were mutilations and interpolations throughout the text.[13] In this critical work which required skilled judgment as well as erudition Erasmus did a very commendable job, and his achievement has been acclaimed by Gorce and other modern patristic scholars.[14] He did restore the authentic Jerome. He identified the spurious works and assembled them in a separate volume—volume II. He arranged the genuine writings according to their subject matter: he placed works dealing with instruction and spiritual direction in volume I; he gathered Jerome's polemical letters and *apologiae* and his correspondence with St. Augustine in volume III; he put letters and treatises explaining Holy Scripture in Volume IV. For each of the *epistolae* or essays he gave a short summary or *argumentum*, and he added copious note or *scholia* throughout the text "which still remain," says Gorce, "an unequalled mine for the scholar and commentator on Jerome."[15] The *scholia* in general are explanatory, but in many and in accompanying *antidoti* there are characteristically Erasmian comments on the ways and practices of Christians in his own day that underline the contrast with the example or ideal in the early Church.[16] These pointed criticisms in the *scholia*, we might note, provided a major complaint among Erasmus' Catholic critics at a later date and appear to be chiefly responsible for the re-editing of Jerome's works under Catholic auspices in the latter half of the century—a byproduct, so to speak, of what is termed the Counter Reformation.[17]

Erasmus dedicated the edition to Archbishop William Warham of Canterbury, the Primate of England, who was an old friend and a generous patron, and wrote a most interesting prefatory letter to him, praising the "incomparable" Jerome, "the greatest among the theologians," and expatiating on the problems as well as the need of restoring him and other ancient authors.[18] He had originally intended to dedicate the work to the Medici Pope Leo X, but had inscribed the New Testament which Froben published earlier in the year to him instead. He also included as an introduction in volume I a life of St. Jerome which has been hailed as "one of the finest examples of Erasmus' scholarly work" and as the first modern or critical biography of the saint.[19] Basing his sketch firmly on the evidence in Jerome's own writings, he broke with the legendary and fictitious and attempted to give a truly historical portrait, though his defense and praise of Jerome leave no doubt of his great admiration for him. Professor Ferguson has called the life "a labor of love, an act of filial piety by one who considered himself Jerome's spiritual descendant."[20] Indeed we may say that the whole edition was such a labor—and the fitting complement of the New Testament which had just appeared, for in Erasmus' eyes Jerome embodied pre-eminently the philosophy of Christ whose true source was Holy Scripture.[21]

The Jerome *Opera* were revised twice during Erasmus' lifetime. Froben brought out a new edition in 1524–26, and Claude Chevallon in Paris published a second revised edition in 1533–34. Again Erasmus' particular province was the letters, and there are corrections and changes in organization, text, and *scholia*, as well as the addition of new prefaces.[22] The Froben firm reprinted the second revised edition in 1536–37, 1553, and 1556, and there are separate printings of the letters and of Erasmus' life of St. Jerome. An extensive topical index to the entire first edition including the *scholia* was prepared by Johann Oecolampadius, the future reformer at Basel, and published in a folio volume by Froben in 1520. Another reformer, Conrad Pellican, prepared a similar index for the second edition in 1526. Until Vittori's Roman edition of St. Jerome began to appear in 1565, Erasmus' held sway and represents one of his most important contributions to the thought and learning of his time.

It is not surprising that the next Father to claim Erasmus' attention as an editor was St. Augustine. The most prolific and profound of all the Latin Fathers, his influence as well as his authority through the Middle Ages and down to Erasmus and his times were hardly surpassed.[23] A critical edition of his many works was the logical complement to the great edition of St. Jerome. Johann Amerbach had published the first nearly complete *Opera omnia* in 1506, and there were printed editions of numerous individual works (and of works falsely attributed to him) long before that, but there was need for an improved edition of the authentic Augustine such as Erasmus alone would be capable of producing.[24] "I was for a long time beseeched," Erasmus tells us, "by the persistent demands of the learned to do for all the books of St. Augustine what I had done for the letters of Jerome."[25] It appears that by mid-1517 Froben was making plans for such an edition and had begun to involve Erasmus in the project, and we know that by the following year the famous scholar had set to work on the task.[26]

The job of authenticating, collating, and emending Augustine was indeed a formidable one, and progress proceeded fitfully and reluctantly. Erasmus declares that he was deterred by the "enormous magnitude of the undertaking."[27] At any rate he was soon diverted by other concerns and publishing ventures, several of which involved editing other Fathers of the Church. Nevertheless, he worked intermittently on the Augustine edition. He sought the help of others, and in 1520 he persuaded the Spanish humanist Juan Luis Vives to edit and annotate *The City of God*.[28] Froben published this volume in September 1522—a large folio of more than 800 pages with extensive notes by Vives and a preface by Erasmus outlining an eventual seven-volume edition of the *Opera* of St. Augustine and defending Vives' commentaries against critics who were angry at the replacement of earlier notes to the famous treatise.[29] The edition also has the relatively rare distinction up to that time of indicating the manuscripts used in preparing the published text: one was lent by the dean of St. Donatian's at Bruges, another belonged to the Carmelites there, and a third Erasmus procured from Cologne. Unfortunately the huge volume did not sell very well, apparently because of its high price, and for the next few years the Augustine project was in abeyance. Froben, however, still wanted to bring out a new edition, and prevailed upon a not very eager Erasmus in 1524 and again in 1527 to resume work on the enterprise. Finally, in the fall of 1527, just prior to the death of Johann Froben, the first two volumes of the Augustine *Opera* came off the press. It was completed in 1529, and the massive set ran to ten folio volumes.

Erasmus dedicated the edition to Archbishop Alfonso Fonseca of Toledo, the Primate of Spain, and prefaced the *Opera* with a long letter to him, extolling the saint so richly endowed with all the gifts of the Holy Spirit and discussing the problems of emending his writings and producing the edition at hand.[30] He concluded the letter with a brief eulogy of Fonseca which stressed his support of humanist studies and reform and linked him in this cause with John Fisher of Rochester and William Warham of Canterbury. Erasmus counted Fonseca among his most important Spanish friends, and the dedication to him obviously was to acknowledge and express thanks for the Archbishop's backing at a time when he was under severe attack in Spain.[31] He also sent presentation copies to other highly placed Spanish friends—to the Archbishop of Seville and Grand Inquisitor Alfonso Manrique, and to the Chancellor of Castile Gattinara. Inaugurated as it was by Vives' text of *The City of God*, the edition may be said to have a Spanish character, and I found it quite in keeping with this aspect to read that St. Ignatius Loyola at a later date was very pleased to receive an edition of Augustine's works, an edition which I assume must have been Erasmus'.[32]

Augustine's works were grouped in the ten volumes according to their general character or content—letters, instructional treatises, polemical writings, etc. Erasmus contributed no *scholia* as he had for Jerome, but there are captions, occasional *censurae*, and extensive marginal notes which give a variety of information—scriptural and other literary references, brief summaries, variant readings, Greek words. Vives' text of *The City of God*, after some hesitation, was reprinted as volume V in the new set in December 1529 and was the last volume to come off the press. (Only the bare text, slightly revised by Erasmus, was reproduced; the prefaces and notes of the 1522 edition were dropped.) There is no doubt that the edition, "a work of immense labor and expense," as Erasmus described it, is an impressive one.[33] Criticisms, of course, can be made from the standpoint of a later scholarship (Erasmus worked too rapidly, he did not consult sufficient manuscripts), but in his own time he served Augustine well, and so eminent an authority as Joseph de Ghellinck tells us that his edition of Augustine "marked an indisputable progress which the competence of the humanist alone made possible" over the earlier edition of Amerbach.[34]

Claude Chevallon published a second edition of the huge set in Paris in late 1531. Chevallon had approached Erasmus four years previously on hearing of the death of Johann Froben and had asked him to supervise such an edition for his establishment, but Erasmus replied that he was obligated to the Frobens and that the presses for Augustine had already begun to clang.[35] The Parisian printer bided his time, and when the new edition came out in 1529 he immediately set about revising it and preparing his own publication. A German scholar, Jacob Haemer of Stuttgart, served as editor and corrected Erasmus' text by collating it with manuscripts borrowed from the library of the Abbey of St. Victor in Paris. Haemer added a dedicatory preface to the Abbot of St. Victor, but Erasmus' dedication to Fonseca was also retained, and the edition was substantially his. The Froben firm brought out a revision in 1543, undertaken by Martin Lypsius, a Louvain Augustinian and close friend of Erasmus who had assisted him with the original Basel edition, and there were subsequent Froben editions in 1555, 1569, and 1579, as well as one published by Chevallon's widow in Paris in 1555.[36] Though others over the years may have contributed to the enterprise, it was essentially Erasmus' achievement, and as his work it remained standard until it was super-seded at least in Catholic Europe by the great edition of Augustine which Plantin published in 1576–77.[37]

Between the Jerome of 1516 and the complete Augustine of 1529 Erasmus produced several other important patristic editions, each one of which has its occasion, significance, and printing history. We shall not discuss these (as well as those which came after 1529) in any detail here, but I should like to enumerate them at least and touch on a few of their most salient features. Each deserves fuller consideration in an adequate appraisal of Erasmus' life's work, and we can but underline this point at the present time.

In February 1520 Froben published Erasmus' edition of the writings of St. Cyprian. A folio volume of over 500 pages, it was a marked improve-ment over the preceding Paris edition of Cyprian in 1512, for Erasmus not only used additional manuscripts to emend the text or show variant readings (in the margin), but he added several treatises not previously published, and he identified and separated works wrongly attributed to Cyprian.[38] Erasmus subsequently produced for the Frobens three revised editions—in November 1521, in 1525, and in 1530—and there were also numerous reprints of the work. Next came an edition of Arnobius the Younger's Commentaries on the Psalms which Froben published as a small folio in September 1522 at the same time as *The City of God*. This was an *editio princeps* based on a manuscript recently discovered and sent to Erasmus by a friend, Maternus Hatten, who was vicar of the cathedral of Speyer. To it was added "as a bonus, so to speak," Erasmus' own com-mentary on the second Psalm. The edition was dedicated to the new but short-lived Pope Adrian VI.[39]

Early the following year Erasmus' edition of the works of St. Hilary of Poitiers appeared, correcting and improving the edition of Robert For-tuné which had been published by Badius in Paris in 1511. One of the most notable features of this publication was Erasmus' prefatory letter or ded-ication to Jean de Carondelet, a high official at the Hapsburg court in the Low Countries.[40] Erasmus at this time was deeply concerned about the influence of his critics, particularly at Louvain, who were connecting him with Luther and blaming him for the dissidence and heresy that had be-come so widespread, and he sought the understanding and support of im-portant people. Carondelet, a devoted friend and a very influential figure in Hapsburg circles, was a logical person to address, and Erasmus used the model of Hilary confronting the Arians of the fourth century, or at least the occasion of that doctrinal struggle, to clarify and substantiate his own position in the Lutheran controversy. Throughout the preface the stress is on being moderate and irenic, on not defining excessively or going beyond what Holy Scripture warrants, and such Erasmian *dicta* as "the sum and substance of our religion is peace and concord" and "once faith was more a matter of a way of life than of a profession of articles" are enunciated.[41] The letter was a major statement of the Erasmian point of view, and indeed the whole edition affords a most interesting example of how Erasmus in the context of the religious crisis drew on the patristic heritage for guidance and support.[42] His employment of Hilary, however, did not disarm his critics. In fact, the preface gave rise to new accusations against him, and several passages or propositions from it were condemned by the Sorbonne in 1526 and were hotly debated at the Valladolid conference which examined Erasmus' work in 1527.[43]

Aside from the revision of Jerome's letters, no new edition of the Fathers appeared in 1524. In 1525, however, came the first of a series of volumes containing the works of St. John Chrysostom, the first Greek Father Erasmus will edit and publish, and an author of whom he appears particularly desirous of having good texts at this time.[44] In April Froben brought out the treatise *De orando Deum* in Erasmus' Latin translation along with the Greek, and in May he printed the Greek text only of Chrysostom's *De sacerdotio*. These were followed by additional works of Chrysostom's in 1526 and 1527, including a large folio of collected writings in Latin translation together with selected works of St. Athanasius which Erasmus translated and published for the first time.[45] The climax was reached with a five-volume Latin edition of Chrysostom which the Froben press published in 1530. This in turn was revised and enlarged, with Erasmus' assistance, and published in Paris by Claude Chevallon in 1536 a short time prior to Erasmus' death.[46] Both editions were prefaced by a brief life of St. John Chrysostom by Erasmus.

Meanwhile Erasmus had published his great Augustine and several other early Fathers. In 1526 he brought out the first printed edition of St. Irenaeus' *Adversus haereses*, the text being a collation of three manuscripts, with variant readings amply noted in the margins.[47] He revised this work for publication in 1528 and again in 1534. A year after the Irenaeus came a four-volume folio edition of St. Ambrose, published first by Froben and then by Chevallon in Paris in early 1529. This substantial edition of the *Opera*, which Erasmus dedicated to Archbishop Jan Laski, the Primate of Poland, supplanted the earlier edition of Amerbach (1492) and was fuller and more critically edited, with Erasmus identifying spurious works and giving a number of variant readings in the margin.[48] Next came the Augustine, accompanied in March 1529 by a short treatise of Lactantius', *De opificio Dei*, which Erasmus edited by correcting the earlier Aldine text, and annotated with rather extensive *scholia* for the first few chapters.[49]

1530 saw the five-volume Chrysostom, then in 1531 came an edition of the sermons of St. Gregory Nazianzen which had been translated into Latin by Willibald Pirckheimer, the noted Nuremberg humanist. Pirckheimer had died in December 1530, and Erasmus at his request edited the text for the Froben press and wrote a dedication to Duke George of Saxony.[50] Chevallon, as was so often his custom, reissued the work in Paris the next year. In 1532 the Froben firm brought out Erasmus' edition of the writings of St. Basil in Greek. This was a large folio volume, dedicated to Jacopo Sadoleto, Bishop of Carpentras and a distinguished scholar himself, and it has the distinction of being the first Greek edition of Basil to be printed.[51] Erasmus followed this work with the publication of his own Latin translations of two of Basil's treatises—one, *De Spiritu Sancto*, at the Froben press, the other, *De laudibus jejunii*, by Faber Emmeus in Freiburg.

Finally in 1536 came the last of Erasmus' patristic editions—his two-volume *Opera omnia* of Origen in Latin translation. This was the last publication to come from his hand, and it was completed and put on the market only after his death. The Froben press as usual produced it with the assistance of an old colleague of Erasmus', Beatus Rhenanus, who wrote the prefatory letter dedicating it, as Erasmus intended, to Hermann von Wied, Archbishop of Cologne. Beatus tells us how Erasmus worked on Origen after having edited Jerome, Cyprian, Augustine, and others, and comments that "sometimes the best are reserved 'til the end"; he also gives us in his preface a moving account of the great humanist's failing health and death and a brief sketch of his life.[52] We might note, however, that although Origen was reserved until last Erasmus had been deeply influenced by him from the start, and considered him the greatest perhaps of all the ancient scriptural exegetes.[53] In listings of the early Fathers (as, for example, in the quotation from the *Ratio verae theologiae* at the beginning of this essay), his name generally heads the list. The edition also contains a short life of Origen by Erasmus and comments on his doctrine and work. The translations for the most part are ancient ones attributed to Rufinus and St. Jerome, but they include one by Erasmus—a fragment of Origen's Commentaries on the Gospel according to Matthew which Froben had originally published in the summer of 1527.[54] The edition superseded the *editio princeps* of Origen's works which Badius first published in Paris in 1512,[55] and it marked a fitting conclusion to the life's work of a man who was so deeply rooted in the patristic tradition and who sought so tirelessly to restore that tradition in the service of learning and the cause of Christian renewal.

NOTES

1. In his *Paraclesis* or introduction to the New Testament he first published in 1516 Erasmus tells us that Christ Himself called His teaching a "rebirth" (he uses the word *renascentia*), and he urges a return to Scripture in order to discover the "philosophy of Christ." The rebirth reference is obviously to John 3. The *Paraclesis* in translation is in CHR, pp. 92–106.

2. In his letter to Colet Erasmus praises him for striving to restore "that ancient true theology" and pledges that he will join him in this task as soon as he is able. CWE, I, 202–6. For the accolade see Allen, V, 2–3.

3. *Hieronymi opera* (9 vols.; Basel, 1516), II, fol. 2.

4. LB, V, 82. See also *ibid.*, V, 132–34. Compare the passage quoted with Erasmus' defense of Jerome as a theologian in his *Hieronymi Stridonensis vita* in *Erasmi opuscula*, ed. Wallace K. Ferguson (The Hague, 1933), pp. 178–80. Jerome is also likened to a "golden river."

5. CHR, p. 99.

6. Henri de Lubac, s.j., *Exégèse médiévale*, Second Part, II (Paris, 1964), 431.

7. Preserved Smith, *Erasmus, a Study of His Life, Ideals, and Place in History* (New York, 1923), pp. 189–93. The most substantial article on the subject is Denys Gorce, "La Patristique dans la réforme d'Erasme," *Festgabe Joseph Lortz* (2 vols.; Baden-Baden, 1958), I, 233–76, though it focuses on the Jerome edition. The headnotes in Allen to the dedicatory letters for each of the patristic editions contain a wealth of information, and P. S. Allen in his lecture "Erasmus' Services to Learning" in *Erasmus, Lectures and Wayfaring Sketches* (Oxford, 1934), pp. 47–55, has given us a very succinct but excellent précis. The short article by Pierre Petitmengin, "Comment étudier l'activité d'Erasme, éditeur de textes antiques?" in *Colloquia Erasmiana Turonensia* (2 vols.; Toronto, 1972), I, 217–22, is suggestive and has some very good comments on Erasmus as an editor. Charles Béné, *Erasme et Saint Augustin ou l'influence de Saint Augustin sur l'humanisme d'Erasme* (Geneva, 1969), as its subtitle indicates, traces Augustine's influence on Erasmus' thought, but it has little to say about his patristic editions. Erasmus' edition of St. Augustine is analyzed in J. de Ghellinck, *Patristique et moyen âge* (3 vols.; Gembloux, 1946–48), III, 378–92. Facsimiles of Erasmus' prefaces to his patristic editions are published in Desiderius Erasmus, *Prefaces to the Fathers, the New Testament, On Study*, ed. Robert Peters (Menston, England, 1970). Peters has contributed an introduction and has also a brief article, "Erasmus and the Fathers: Their Practical Value," in *Church History*, 36, No. 3 (September 1967), 254–61.

8. Allen, I, 103, 321, 326, 332–33, 353, and CWE, I, 35, 295–96, 302, 305, 308–9.

9. See Georges Chantraine, *"Mystère" et "Philosophie du Christ" selon Erasme* (Namur–Gembloux, 1971), chap. I: "La vocation théologique d'Erasme."

10. *Erasmus, Lectures and Wayfaring Sketches*, p. 124. See also Erasmus' descrip-

tion of his meeting with Froben in Allen, II, 22–23; Beatus Rhenanus' account in his life of Erasmus in CHR, pp. 41–42; and Eileen Bloch, "Erasmus and the Froben Press: The Making of an Editor," *The Library Quarterly*, 35 (1965), 109–20.

11. *Hieronymi opera* (Basel, 1516), V, title^v; Beatus' life of Erasmus in CHR, pp. 41–42; and H. D. Saffrey, "Un humaniste dominicain, Jean Cuno de Nuremberg, précurseur d'Erasme à Bâle," *Bibliothèque d'humanisme et renaissance*, 33 (1971), 19–62.

12. Allen, II, 77, 217. These accounts may be found in Allen, II, 76–77, 215–19, and Margaret Mann Phillips, *The 'Adages' of Erasmus* (Cambridge, 1964), pp. 208–9.

13. See the preface to Jerome's *Opera* in Migne, *Patrologia latina*, 22, xi–xiv. The *editio princeps* of Jerome's *Epistolae* was published by Sweynheym and Pannartz in Rome in 1468. The standard modern edition is that edited by I. Hilberg in *Corpus scriptorum ecclesiasticorum latinorum*, 54–56.

14. Gorce, "La patristique . . . ," 272–76; Ferdinand Cavallera, *Saint Jerome, sa vie et son oeuvre* (2 vols.; Louvain–Paris, 1922), II, 146; and *Saint Jerome, Lettres*, ed. and trans. Jerome Labourt (8 vols.; Paris, 1949–64), I, li.

15. Gorce, "La patristique . . . ," 273.

16. Roland H. Bainton, *Erasmus of Christendom* (New York, 1969), pp. 132–33, gives two good examples of these comments. I should like to note a few others. In *Hieronymi opera*, I, fol. 76^v, Erasmus observes in a *scholium* touching on papal authority during Jerome's time that "in another letter Jerome asserted that once all bishops were equal to one another." Interestingly, this sentence was dropped in the 1524 revised edition of Jerome's *Opera* (see I, fol. 186, of this edition), although Erasmus had made the same point in an *antidotus* in III, fol. 150^v, of the 1516 edition and retained it in the 1524 edition (see II, fol. 335). In a *scholium* in IV, fol. 13, he states that "it should be noted that Jerome calls Damasus the highest priest [*summum sacerdotem*] and not supreme pontiff [*summum pontificem*]." In the copy of the 1516 edition of Jerome's *Opera* which I have used an alert reader who with pen in hand was reading through this massive work from 1518 to 1521 wrote at this point in the margin: "Papa non est summum pontificem" (sic). Thus a notation of Erasmus' struck a responsive note!

17. The Catholic replacement for Erasmus' edition was the revision by Marianus Victorius, or Vittori, published by Paulus Manutius at Rome in nine volumes in 1565–72 and subsequently by Christophe Plantin at Antwerp. It is crystal clear from the title page of volume I and the dedication to Pius IV that it was produced to confute and supplant Erasmus who is viewed throughout in the darkest light. The first Jesuit author, Peter Canisius, also edited and published a single volume of selected letters of Jerome, to which he appended a preface, dated 1565, taking sharp issue with Erasmus' *scholia*. He wished that Erasmus had confined himself to editing Jerome without injecting his "poisonous" remarks. There were many editions of this smaller work which was based on Vittori.

18. Allen, II, 211–21, and CWE, III, 254–66.

19. Wallace K. Ferguson in *Erasmi opuscula*, p. 129, and Cavallera, *Saint Jerome*, II, 145–46, respectively. The life (with a brief introduction) is in *Erasmi opuscula*, pp. 125–90. See also John B. Maguire, "Erasmus' Biographical Masterpiece: *Hieronymi Stridonensis Vita*," *Renaissance Quarterly*, 26, No. 3 (Autumn 1973), 265–73.

20. *Erasmi opuscula*, p. 125.

21. In his life of Jerome Erasmus asks: "Who had a more thorough knowledge of the philosophy of Christ? Who expressed it more vigorously either in literature or in life?" (*Erasmi opuscula*, p. 179).

22. Allen, V, 492–93, and X, 144–47.

23. P. O. Kristeller, "Augustine and the Early Renaissance," *Studies in Renaissance Thought and Letters* (Rome, 1956), pp. 355–72, and Béné, *Erasme et Saint Augustin.*

24. De Ghellinck, *Patristique et moyen âge*, III, 368–77. Sweynheym and Pannartz, for instance, had published the *editio princeps* of *The City of God* in 1467, and Amerbach himself had published that work in 1489.

25. Allen, V, 118. These are the opening words of Erasmus' preface to the *De civitate Dei* Froben published in 1522. Urban Rieger's letter quoted above is an example of these "demands."

26. Allen, II, 557–58, and III, 337. On the general background of the Augustine edition see Allen, V, 117–18, and VIII, 146–47, and de Ghellinck, *Patristique et moyen âge*, III, 378ff.

27. Allen, V, 118.

28. See Vives' preface to his commentaries, *De civitate Dei* (Basel, 1522), and also Carlos G. Noreña, *Juan Luis Vives* (The Hague, 1970), pp. 130–37.

29. Erasmus' preface is in Allen, V, 118–21. Vives in a separate preface entitled *De veteribus interpretibus huius operis* also defends his commentaries against these critics and discusses the earlier annotations, chiefly those of two English Dominicans, Trevet and Waleys.

30. Allen, VIII, 147–61. On Fonseca see Allen, VI, 410.

31. See Marcel Bataillon, *Erasme et l'Espagne* (Paris, 1937), pp. 253ff.

32. Hugo Rahner, *Ignatius the Theologian* (New York, 1968), p. 36. The only other complete Augustine up to that time was Amerbach's.

33. Allen, VII, 182.

34. De Ghellinck, *Patristique et moyen âge*, III, 387.

35. Allen, V, 118, and VIII, 146–47, and Allen, *Erasmus, Lectures and Wayfaring Sketches*, pp. 130–31. After Johann Froben's death in October 1527 his son Jerome continued the firm, for a brief time with his stepfather, Johann Herwagen, and then with his brother-in-law, Nicholas Episcopius.

36. On Martin Lypsius see Allen, III, 185–86.

37. On Plantin's edition of Augustine *per theologos Lovanienses* see de Ghellinck, *Patristique et moyen âge*, III, 392–403.

38. Allen, IV, 23–24. On the Paris edition see Eugene F. Rice, "The Humanist Idea of Christian Antiquity: Lefèvre d'Etaples and his Circle," *Studies in the Renaissance*, 9 (1962), 156–60.

39. Allen, V, 99–111.

40. Allen, V, 172–92. On Jean de Carondelet see Allen, III, 257. The actual copy of the edition which Erasmus inscribed and sent to Carondelet is in Harvard's Houghton Library; its title page appears as an illustration in this volume. An English translation of the prefatory letter of dedication to Carondelet is published as the Appendix in this volume. For further comment on this letter and the Hilary edition see John C. Olin, "Erasmus and His Edition of St. Hilary," *Erasmus in English*, 9 (1978), 8–11.

41. See Appendix, below.

42. Cf. Peter G. Bietenholz, *History and Biography in the Work of Erasmus of Rotterdam* (Geneva, 1966), pp. 33–37.

43. *Collectio judiciorum de novis erroribus*, ed. Charles du Plessis d'Argentré (3 vols.; Paris, 1728–36), II, 73–77, and Bataillon, *Erasme et l'Espagne*, pp. 272–78.

44. On the Chrysostom series see Allen, VI, 44–45, and IX, 3–4. See also Phillips, *The 'Adages' of Erasmus*, p. 185, where (in an addition to the adage 'Festina lente' inserted in 1526) Erasmus speaks of the need to have good Greek and Latin texts of so great a doctor. Actually Froben had published in 1518 and 1519 a very short commentary wrongly attributed to St. Basil which Erasmus had translated from the Greek. Aside from this, Chrysostom was first.

45. The dedication to King John III of Portugal which prefaces the Chrysostom portion of the joint Chrysostom–Athanasius volume published in March 1527 is notable and has an interesting history. See Allen, VI, 483–91, and Marcel Bataillon, *Etudes sur le Portugal au temps de l'humanisme* (Coimbra, 1952), pp. 70ff.

46. Allen, IX, 4.

47. Allen, VI, 384, and José Ruysschaert, "Le manuscrit 'Romae Descriptum' de l'edition érasmienne d'Irénée de Lyon," *Scrinium Erasmianum*, ed. J. Coppens (2 vols.; Leiden, 1969), I, 263–76.

48. Allen, VII, 118–19. The title page, volume I, advises: "Examine, reader, and you will find another Ambrose than the one you formerly had."

49. Allen, VIII, 61.

50. Allen, IX, 266–68, and Lewis W. Spitz, *The Religious Renaissance of the German Humanists* (Cambridge, Mass., 1963), p. 196.

51. Allen, IX, 435. I note that Julien Garnier, the later Maurist editor of St. Basil, says in the preface of his edition (3 vols.; Paris, 1721) that as he worked on Basil he always kept Erasmus' edition before his eyes.

52. Allen, I, 52–56.

53. See *The Enchiridion of Erasmus*, trans. Raymond Himelick (Bloomington, 1963), pp. 53, 78–79, 107, and André Godin, "De Vitrier à Origène: Recherches sur la patristique érasmienne," *Colloquium Erasmianum* (Mons, 1968), pp. 48–57.

54. Allen, VII, 101.

55. On the printing and impact of Origen in these years see Edgar Wind, "The Revival of Origen," *Studies in Art and Literature for Belle da Costa Greene*, ed. D. Miner (Princeton, 1954), pp. 412–24, and D. P. Walker, "Origène en France au début du XVIe siècle," *Courants religieux et humanisme à fin du XVe et au début du XVIe siècle* (Paris, 1959), pp. 101–19.

4

THE PRAISE OF FOLLY

> Between what matters and what seems to matter,
> how should the world we know judge wisely?

This query which begins E. C. Bentley's *Trent's Last Case* can also serve to open our discussion of Erasmus' most famous and most enigmatic work, *Moriae encomium* or *The Praise of Folly*. The title itself is a pun and a paradox. Erasmus tells us in his dedication of the book to Thomas More that More's family name suggested the theme, the Greek word for folly being μωρία, although More himself was as far from folly as his name was near to the Greek word. And, he continues, he knew that More would enjoy this *jeu d'esprit* of his, since More took delight in humor of this kind. Erasmus was aware, however, that he had not written simply a humorous essay, a comic encomium. From the outset he entertained, we may surmise, a more serious purpose, or at least he saw the ironic and satiric possibilities inherent in a disquisition on folly and the ambiguity of the term itself. St. Paul's first letter to the Corinthians would have revealed to him the profound ambivalence of the concept of folly, if indeed he needed any instruction. God has confounded the wise by the folly of the cross. What, then, is folly? How do we discern what is foolish and what is wise? How do we understand St. Paul's paradoxical transposition?

It is along the line of these questions, it seems to me, that Erasmus' celebrated essay should be read. I do not mean to detract from the fun and good humor of the essay by emphasizing too serious an approach. It does begin in a frolicsome spirit, and a jocular note is frequently struck throughout. Indeed the entire piece purports to be a declamation by light-hearted Folly who is personified as a goddess and who is literally praising herself. The form of the essay is whimsical and amusing. Yet the ambivalence and the paradox remain. As Erasmus clearly indicates in his dedication to More, his encomium has not been altogether foolish. Irony will often prevail, truths will be spoken, penetrating observations on life's comedy will be made, and Erasmus himself will speak critically and straightforwardly through the mask of Folly. Thus there is considerable variety of tone and meaning in Folly's declamation. The task for the listener–reader is to recognize the intonation and to interpret correctly what Folly has to say. It is not as simple a task as one may think, and from the moment of its first publication the book generated differing interpretations, not to say gross misunderstanding and deep-seated indignation. Erasmus' plight in this regard calls to mind the comment of Ronald Knox about G. K. Chesterton that "he is rash enough to combine humor not merely with satire but with serious writing; and that, it is well known, is a thing the public will not stand."[1]

Before we come to grips with the problem of interpretation, however, let us review a few basic facts about the essay and sketch its general outline. Erasmus wrote *The Praise of Folly* in Thomas More's home at Bucklersbury in the heart of London in late summer 1509. He had just returned from a long stay in Italy and had come back to England at the urging of his English friends with the expectation of generous support for his scholarly endeavors. As a guest of More's he composed the little work to amuse himself and occupy his time while he recovered from an attack of kidney stone.[2] It delighted his friends, and later they arranged (so he says) to have the book published in France. Actually it was Erasmus himself who undertook its publication and saw it through the press of Gilles de Gourmont in Paris in June or July 1511.[3] It was soon published at Strasburg and Antwerp and again at Paris, and it became what we might call a best seller. Johann Froben at Basel brought out an enlarged edition in 1515, with extensive notes to clarify the text by Gerard Lister, and he published another important revision in 1522. About forty editions were published in Erasmus' lifetime. A first English translation by Sir Thomas Chaloner appeared in London in 1549.[4] It became unquestionably one of Erasmus' most popular and most enduring works.

The book, as we have already indicated, professes to be a discourse in praise of folly delivered by a garrulous woman—actually a goddess—who personifies that light-headed quality of mind and spirit. It is Folly thus who is speaking in the essay and praising herself—a feature of the book which gives rise to the same confusion about the validity of what is being said as the conundrum that a Cretan declares that all Cretans are liars. The address starts out humorously in the manner of a learned parody, an erudite but mock encomium. It takes on a more serious tone as it progresses and is often ironic. In the middle of the harangue Folly launches a vehement attack on hairsplitting theologians, pharisaical monks, and other miscreants. This section is one of the most memorable parts of the book and has generally been viewed as the very heart of the piece and, if we may mix our metaphors, its cutting edge.[5] At the end Folly praises a higher wisdom which in this passing world is deemed foolish, and her mock encomium and her satire turn into the genuine praise of "Christian folly." Quite obviously the goddess does not adhere to a steady and consistent line.

But is there a method or pattern in Folly's declamation or does it suffer from what has been called "a fundamental incoherence"?[6] Folly herself tells us that she speaks extempore, and concluding she calls her discourse a hodgepodge of words. Despite the disclaimer, however, I believe that we can discern a definite thematic and structural unity in the book. I hope that the following analysis will give evidence of it. The work can be divided into three main parts, preceded by a short introduction, and ending with a very brief peroration. In the introduction Folly announces herself, informs her listeners about what she is going to do, and tells them of her parents and birth. (She is the daughter of Plutus and the nymph Youthfulness and was born in the utopian Islands of the Blest.) In part one, which is the longest section of the book, she speaks of the gifts and blessings she bestows on mankind. Her attitude is mostly nonsensical and ironic. She praises the ignorance, illusion, and stupidity which in her view make life tolerable and indeed enjoyable for men, but intermixed in this mock or paradoxical encomium are penetrating observations and insights as well as a passage of sharp criticism of certain religious superstitions or follies. We can readily recognize the voice of Erasmus speaking in these latter instances. In part two the goddess presents her disciples and followers, that is, men from important walks of life who worship her not in temples or with ceremonial offerings but with true devotion in their own daily lives—schoolmasters, grammarians, writers, lawyers, theologians, monks, princes, prelates, popes. "Heavens, what a farce it is, what a motley crowd of fools," she explains, but her comment in this part gradually loses its light or ironic touch and becomes deadly serious in its castigation of those "fools" whose self-love and self-deception are detestable and whose lives are a scandal and disgrace. The reformer completely overtakes the jesting observer of the human scene. In part three Folly briefly returns to her light-hearted mood and begins to quote ancient authorities who had something favorable to say about her. She quickly comes to Holy Scripture, and then with particular reference to St. Paul's first letter to the Corinthians she launches into a discussion of "the folly of the cross" and of the kinship between Christianity and Platonism in the store they set on higher, spiritual things. The sincerity and earnestness of this final portion of her declamation are unmistakable.

How do we relate or unite these three parts? What is their principle of *concordia*? It seems quite obvious that various meanings of folly supply a bond or, to put it in another way, that in each part a different kind of fool holds the center of the stage. Part one treats folly as a mindless or uncritical attitude toward life—that is, as foolishness in the conventional sense—and the happy moron, or at best the instinctive, unthinking man, is ironically extolled. In part two a major shift occurs. Folly becomes something morally reprehensible. Stupidity and self-deception now involve the betrayal of a trust and have harmful consequences in society. The fool here pictured in the central portion of the book is a knave, an evildoer, a dangerous man, and he is not extolled but satirized and condemned. In part three folly takes on still another meaning, one quite contrary to those that had been previously employed. It is now the Pauline-Platonic rejection of this world's standards, it is the spiritual wisdom of the Christian who seeks a goal beyond this material world. "We are fools for Christ's sake," says St. Paul, and Folly in her concluding remarks truly praises this kind of fool.

The abrupt change of meaning and of mood may seem confusing at first, but we can soon perceive, I believe, a purpose or logic in it. This lies in the juxtaposition of the different types of fool and in the relationships between them. The moron or unthinking man (of part one) has an affinity with the genuine Christian (of part three) to the extent that in both cases the rule of reason has ceased to apply. One acts out of instinct, the other out of faith, and both are quite removed from the practical, prudential world of affairs. Both seek happiness, and both attain to an inner freedom. Both are praised for having a "higher" wisdom, though in the first case the eulogy is a mock one and in the latter, of course, the eulogy is genuine. Their resemblance perhaps is not really substantial, for the ignoramus or happy moron does not rise above his sense appetites and material concerns, but there is a curious surface similarity between the two, the ambiguity of which cannot fail to intrigue us. Perhaps the Christian fool (of part three) is actually the sublimation of the natural fool (of part one).[7] Perhaps the natural fool is a crude version—a rough prototype, so to speak —of the Christian fool. Perhaps this analogy echoes the dictum that grace builds on nature, a dictum which is a basic assumption in Erasmus' thought.

The wicked fool (of part two) on the other hand stands in sharp contrast to these other two types and serves as their foil. He is not out of step with the established order, and his vanity and conceit delude him into thinking that he is wise. He is the reverse of the other two in the evil and harm that he does. Erasmus' description of him in the many guises he assumes—and these are in the upper ranks of society—gives the book its reform thrust. At the same time it reveals the ambivalence of the attitude of the natural fool toward life and its responsibilities, and it heightens the worth and significance of the Christian fool and his view of life. Thus the presence of the knave or villain in the middle of Folly's discourse is both pivotal to the development of Erasmus' theme and essential to the overall plan and purpose of the book. It bears out above all Erasmus' argument in his letter to Martin Dorp that his intentions in *The Praise of Folly* were the same as in his other works, although the method which he used was different.[8]

The triad, then, of natural fool, wicked fool, and Christian fool forms a meaningful unity and gives the essay a dramatic structural pattern, but there is more to Erasmus' little masterpiece than simply this, however important it may be. This "more" subsists deep in the peculiar character of the work and cuts across the structural divisions we have discussed. The title, the dedication, the literary form and device employed as well as frequent passages throughout the book remind us that Folly's declamation runs contrary to the normal order of things and is somehow topsy-turvy, that a reversal of values has occurred and accepted opinions have been turned upside down. And the fact that it is Folly who is speaking is a problem which confronts us at every point. How are we to take her words? Is she telling us the truth or talking nonsense? Is she deceiving or instructing us? The ambiguity is never quite resolved. We are not always sure about Folly's declarations.

It is to this pervasive quality of the work that we refer when we say it is ironic or paradoxical. Both terms signify that the real meaning of what is being written or said lies well beneath the surface and may in fact be the opposite of what is apparently expressed. A seeming contradiction may be involved, a hidden message may be conveyed. This mode of speech is very ancient. It is found in Scripture as well as in the classics, and the Greek satirist Lucian, one of Erasmus' (and More's) favorite authors, was a past master of such rhetorical techniques. This mode or style also reflects an attitude toward life—a perception of its ambiguity and an awareness of the gap between appearances and reality. Erasmus was preoccupied with this discordance and with the distorting and reversing of values that accompany it, and whatever else it is *The Praise of Folly* is a *jeu d'esprit*, a witty verbal game, on this theme. But it is also a serious and satiric discourse on man and his behavior, even "a study in speculation about the nature of man," as it has been called.[9] The combination itself is paradoxical—a *coincidentia oppositorum*—and thus it is in keeping with the whole spirit and form of the work.

We are now back to where we were at the beginning of this essay, that is, at the point of stressing the ambiguity of Folly's declamation and the questions of meaning which Erasmus' book has raised. These features of the encomium mirror the ambiguity and puzzle of life itself, and we come to grips with them in terms of our own approach to life and the scale of values we accept. It is here, it seems to me, that St. Paul's famous transposition of wisdom and folly in the first letter to the Corinthians is most relevant.[10] Erasmus has simply extended and elaborated this Pauline paradox. The conventional wisdom of the world has ceased to be the operative standard throughout Folly's address, for, as St. Paul says, "the wisdom of this world is folly in God's sight." There is a Platonic character also to this way of seeing and thinking, and a symbol or image from one of the Platonic dialogues gives us another clue, I believe, to the understanding of *The Praise of Folly*. The image is the carved Silenus figure to which Alcibiades likened Socrates in the last part of the *Symposium*. A Silenus in this context is a statuette rough and ugly in appearance but so constructed that it can be opened to reveal a finely carved and beautiful figure inside. Its outward form belies its inward grace. Like Socrates Folly is a Silenus—or at least she is in a good portion of *The Praise of Folly*— and her words too like those of Socrates resemble these deceptive figurines. They may seem ridiculous at first hearing, but, to quote Alcibiades, "whoever penetrates and analyses them will discover first of all that they are the most inspired and contain the greatest number of moral parables, and finally that they possess the widest scope and comprise the whole duty of the man aiming to be good and beautiful."[11]

The Sileni of Alcibiades were proverbial, and Erasmus wrote an important essay in his *Adagia* of 1515 with that title.[12] He obviously saw this image as a very appropriate expression of his own preoccupation with the disparity between what appears to be and what actually is. Folly in the first part of her declamation uses this Platonic simile. Taking credit for most of life's blessings she lays claim paradoxically to the virtue of prudence. This leads her to a discussion of what genuine prudence is and of how the wise man is deceived in thinking he possesses it. She argues:

> In the first place, it's well known that all human affairs are like the figures of Silenus described by Alcibiades and have two completely opposite faces, so that what is death at first sight, as they say, is life if you look within, and vice versa, life is death. The same applies to beauty and ugliness, riches and poverty, obscurity and fame, learning and ignorance, strength and weakness, the noble and the base-born, happy and sad, good and bad fortune, friend and foe, healthy and harmful—in fact you'll find everything

suddenly reversed if you open the Silenus. Maybe some of you will think I've expressed this too philosophically; well, I'll speak bluntly, as the saying goes, to make myself clear. We all agree a king is rich and powerful, but if he lacks all spiritual goods nothing belongs to him, and he's surely the poorest of men. And if he's addicted to a large number of vices he's no more than a cheap slave. We could philosophize about others in the same way, but one example will suffice.[13]

She quickly adds that the whole life of man is a play and that we should not peer behind the masks and destroy the illusion. Prudence dictates that we must not probe too far. The shift is typical of Folly's argumentation and of Erasmus' literary and intellectual sinuosity. There may be a certain truth in this latter point of view, but the main thrust of the passage is the comparison of human affairs with the Sileni of Alcibiades. Folly stresses that appearances deceive us, that our estimate of things is frequently reversed. "Hence [so Erasmus declares in his "Sileni Alcibiadis"] gold is more valued than learning, ancient lineage more than virtue, the gifts of the body more than the endowments of the mind, ceremonies are put before true piety, the rules of men before the teachings of Christ, the mask is preferred to the truth, the shadow to the reality, the counterfeit to the genuine, the fleeting to the substantial, the momentary to the eternal."[14] Folly in her own person illustrates this theme. Indeed her whole encomium may be called a sermon on this text and an exercise for her listener or reader in judging wisely what she has to say.

NOTES

1. *Essays in Satire* (New York, 1930), p. 39. The first extended criticism of *The Praise of Folly* came from the Louvain theologian Martin Dorp. See Allen, II, 10–16. Erasmus replied in a long letter to Dorp in May 1515, explaining and defending his work, and Thomas More also wrote to Dorp in defense of Erasmus and *The Praise of Folly* a few months later. For Erasmus' letter see CHR, pp. 55–91; for More's letter see *St. Thomas More: Selected Letters*, ed. E. F. Rogers (New Haven, 1961), pp. 8–64. Both letters are extremely valuable in understanding Erasmus' aim and method in *The Praise of Folly*. For other criticisms of Erasmus see Myron P. Gilmore, "Italian Reactions to Erasmian Humanism," in *Itinerarium Italicum*, edd. Heiko A. Oberman and Thomas A. Brady, Jr. (Leiden, 1975), pp. 61–115.

2. I am following the account Erasmus gives in his letter to Dorp in 1515. The exact details concerning its composition and first publication are not too clear. In the famous sketch of Thomas More which he sent to Ulrich von Hutten in 1519 Erasmus tells us that More was responsible for his writing the work. See Allen, IV, 16.

3. Allen, I, 19 and 459.

4. This translation has been edited by Clarence H. Miller and published by the

Early English Text Society (Oxford, 1965). Several modern English translations are also available: Hoyt Hudson's (Princeton, 1941), Leonard F. Dean's (Chicago, 1946), Betty Radice's (Baltimore, 1971). The last-mentioned, published by Penguin Books, has an excellent introduction and notes by A. H. T. Levi and also contains Erasmus' letter to Dorp. I should like also to call attention to a facsimile publication of Froben's important edition of 1515 (introduction by H. A. Schmid; Basel, 1931). The original copy of the facsimile edition belonged to Oswald Myconius and contains numerous marginal drawings by the young Hans Holbein.

5. Erasmus' criticism of theologians and monks was greatly expanded in the 1515 Froben edition.

6. A. E. Douglas argues the latter case in *Erasmus*, ed. T. A. Dorey (Albuquerque, 1970), pp. 45ff.

7. In a brief passage toward the end of the book Erasmus seems to say as much. He writes: "It is quite clear that the Christian religion has a kind of kinship with folly in some form, though it has none at all with wisdom. If you want proofs of this, first consider the fact that the very young and the very old, women and simpletons, are the people who take the greatest delight in sacred and holy things, and are therefore always found nearest the altars, led there doubtless by their natural instinct. Secondly, you can see how the first great founders of the faith were great lovers of simplicity and bitter enemies of learning. Finally the biggest fools of all appear to be those who have once been wholly possessed by zeal for Christian piety. They squander their possessions, ignore insults, submit to being cheated, make no distinction between friends and enemies, shun pleasure, sustain themselves on fasting, vigils, tears, toil and humiliations, scorn life and desire only death—in short, they seem to be dead to any normal feelings, as if their spirit dwelt elsewhere than in their body. What else can that be but madness? And so we should not be surprised if the apostles were thought to be drunk on new wine, and Festus judged Paul to be mad" (Betty Radice's translation, p. 201).

8. CHR, p. 59. In the analysis I have made above I am indebted to the following: Clarence H. Miller, "Some Medieval Elements and Structural Unity in Erasmus' *The Praise of Folly*," *Renaissance Quarterly*, 27, No. 4 (Winter 1974), 449–511; Geraldine Thompson, *Under Pretext of Praise* (Toronto, 1973), Chap. 2; and Enid Welsford, *The Fool* (London, 1935), pp. 236–42.

9. Geraldine Thompson, op. cit., p. 72.

10. 1 Cor. 1:18–28, 3:18–20, and 4:10.

11. Francis Birrell's & Shane Leslie's translation in The Nonesuch Press edition of Plato's *Symposium*, p. 102. Cf. *The Collected Dialogues of Plato*, edd. Edith Hamilton & Huntington Cairns (Bollingen Series LXXI; New York, 1961), p. 572.

12. The essay is translated in Margaret Mann Phillips, *The 'Adages' of Erasmus* (Cambridge, 1964), pp. 269–96. It is aimed at the reform of the Church, and in it Erasmus compared Christ and the Apostles to Sileni, and prelates and others of his own day who have false standards to Sileni in reverse.

13. Betty Radice's translation in the Penguin *Praise of Folly*, pp. 103–4.

14. Phillips, op. cit., p. 277.

5

INTERPRETING ERASMUS

In approaching the topic of Erasmus and his place in history, I found that an initial question immediately arose. What exactly is "a place in history"? Without allowing myself to become too involved in speculation concerning the nature and meaning of history, I resolved the query by deciding that for all practical purposes "a place in history" simply means the judgment or evaluation rendered by posterity on an important person and on his life and work. The question thus reduced itself in my mind to the subject of what others have thought about Erasmus. And since it is the business chiefly of historians to think—extensively at least and professionally—about the past, my topic centered on what historians have written about Erasmus, on how they have interpreted and appraised his role in the course of events. I have taken this for my theme. We might call it "Erasmus and the historians." Or perhaps it would be more accurate to say "Erasmus in the view of some modern historians," since I intend to limit my subject and select the examples I shall offer from a very considerable body of historical writing. Such, of course, is inevitable. The recent or current literature on Erasmus alone is a very formidable mass. It affords some confirmation perhaps of Colet's famous dictum that the name of Erasmus will never die.

Is this a valid way of tackling the problem of Erasmus' place in history? I think it is, and I offer two very brief arguments in my behalf. One concerns the nature of history itself. History is after all *our knowledge* of the past. A man's place in history then is our understanding or appreciation of his role. There must be, of course, some objectivity, some reasonable grounds, some careful analysis of the available evidence, but the subjective element is very strong, and the historian will approach the past with his own limitations, his own frame of reference, his own sense of relevance and value. He will tell us in the final analysis only what *he thinks* the

Entitled "Erasmus and His Place in History," the original form of this essay was a lecture given at Ithaca College on October 28, 1969; under that title, an earlier version of the present essay appeared in *Erasmus of Rotterdam, A Quincentennial Symposium*, ed. Richard L. De-Molen (New York: Twayne, 1971), pp. 63–76.

contribution or importance of an historical figure is. There may be broad consensus and apparently very firm grounds for the appraisal, but it remains a human judgment subject to correction and revision. In saying this I stress, as you will note, the fact that history is not a static phenomenon or an interpretation fixed for all time. Our topic, then, tends inevitably to become historiographical—that is, a matter of examining the views and evaluations of various historians.

My second argument is of a different character and not quite so cogent. It is from authority. Preserved Smith, the late distinguished professor of history at Cornell and a renowned scholar of the Reformation of two generations ago, wrote a very substantial biography of Erasmus. The final chapter in this work he entitled "The Genius of Erasmus and His Place in History," and he devoted the chapter to the views and opinions of a number of historians and other scholars on Erasmus. I shall follow his lead in this instance and present a comparable but more recent version of history's judgment.

In the case of history's great figures one often finds a variety of judgment and interpretation, and frequently there is sharp division of opinion, even contradictory views, regarding an individual's role or influence. That situation is fairly commonplace. But in Erasmus' case the interpretive variation as well as the controversy is especially marked. It was so in his own day, and it has continued at least to some extent down to ours. There are reasons, of course, which account for this, aside from the limited and subjective character of historical judgment. At the outset I should like to deal briefly with these factors.

For one thing, Erasmus lived and worked in a period of serious religious crisis and schism, the most serious that ever divided western Christendom. We need hardly elaborate on the intensity of this division. As Europe's leading scholar and intellectual light he was involved in these events by virtue of the character of his work, the thrust of his purpose, and his influence. Yet from the start he resisted alignment or identification with any party or faction in the controversy. He had his point of view and his convictions, but he sought to rise above dogmatic argument lest it contribute to division and deepen the breach within the Church. His efforts were directed toward moderating the quarrel and ending the schism that developed. As a result he fell afoul of both extremes. In his *Compendium vitae* of early 1524 he tells us that "the Lutheran tragedy had burdened him with unbearable ill will" and that "he was torn apart by each faction, while he sought to serve the best interests of each."[1] That same year he wrote to his good friend John Fisher, the Bishop of Rochester: "Indeed, I war on three fronts: against these pagan Romans, who are meanly jealous of me; against certain theologians and friars, who use every stone at hand to bring me down; against some rabid Lutherans, who snarl at me because —so they say—I alone delay their own triumphs."[2] Erasmus had his critics before the "Lutheran tragedy," but it was the enormously divisive and polarizing consequences of the controversy that now developed which caught him in the middle and "tore him apart."

There is no need to retell here the story of Erasmus' attitude or role in the midst of the religious crisis.[3] Our intention is simply to call attention to the situation that involved him and to the effect it had on the way men viewed and judged him. Luther, for example, came to despise him. From his early attitude that Erasmus did not "promote the cause of Christ and God's grace sufficiently," Luther progressed to his scathing attack on him as a skeptic who "oozed Lucian from every pore," in his *De servo arbitrio* of 1525.[4] And the Wittenberg prophet in his later years continued to denounce Erasmus as a scoffer, a pagan, and an enemy of the Gospel.[5] The other side was also relentless in its attack on him. He was seen to be in collusion with Luther and to have laid the egg Luther hatched. Jerome Aleander, papal legate to the court of Charles V in 1520-21 and a noted humanist scholar and former friend of Erasmus, denounced him to Rome as the real instigator of the heresy and disorder that now troubled Europe.[6] His writings were judged to be dangerous and subversive and full of error. A climax was reached in this onslaught against him by his Catholic opponents in 1558 when the fierce and frantic Paul IV (once a friend who had encouraged his scholarly endeavors) declared him a heretic *primae classis* and placed all his works on the papal *Index*.[7]

The unhappy situation that engulfed Erasmus was due not only to the schism but also to the character of his thought and the nature of what he had to say. His goal was reform; he did seek to renew theology and the Christian life through a scriptural revival; he did attack those who blocked the way—the theologians of the schools and the mendicant friars whose Christian profession he felt was an empty and shameless thing. But the reform he sought challenged neither basic dogma nor essential institution and could not be equated with the preaching and the thrust of Luther and the Protestants against the entire fabric of the existing Church. Erasmus does not leave us in any doubt about this. Commenting on Luther's teaching in 1524 Erasmus wrote: "This contains many points which I do not follow, many more which I would question and many that, even if it were safe, I should not dare to profess for reasons of conscience."[8] Yet Erasmian reform did strike deep, it did seek change, it did challenge much within the established order. In this sense Erasmus occupied a middle ground in the controversy. As a result neither side could see him as its own, and both extremes viewed him as faithless and disloyal. The attacks that now befell Erasmus had this seemingly ambiguous centrality of his position at their base. And as the schism deepened and widened Erasmus stubbornly maintained his middle ground, at once faithful to his reform ideas, solicitous of the unity of the Church, and conciliatory in the face of the division that had come. He was an anomaly in an age of feverish polarization.

Part of the explanation for Erasmus' peculiar position—his moderation or middle ground or seeming ambiguity—lies deep within his personality. He looked at the world with a certain detachment and with something of a skeptical gaze; he was acutely sensitive to the self-deception and hypocrisy that abounds; he was not given to scholastic definition or magisterial pronouncement; his language does at times seem cautiously qualified and uncertain—*oratio peregrina*; he sensed by nature the frequent complexity and obscurity of the human situation. The Silenus figure whose outward appearance is quite different from its inward reality had deep attraction for him, and irony in one instance, tolerance in another, were the qualities that came most natural to him. This temper of mind or disposition was reinforced by the kind and quality of his religious faith, just as that faith itself was influenced and formed by his natural inclinations. He saw charity as the great Christian virtue and peace and unity among Christians as its most cherished fruit. His "philosophy of Christ" was a practical guide, and it would lead men restored in Christ to the practice of charity and the haven of peace. Assertion or dogmatism, bitterness or hostility, party or strife were not of its essence and indeed were antithetical to the whole spirit and message of the Gospel. These particular emphases of Erasmus' religious faith conformed to the natural bent of his mind, and the personal union thus effected contrived to dissociate him from all factionalism or fanaticism. Erasmus, it was said even in his own day, was "for himself," but in reality he stood, as he gazed out upon the follies of the world, for the Gospel of unity and peace. His moderation or middle ground was rooted in large part in this equation. By the same token it was difficult for men of other tempers and other convictions to understand or accept him.

Erasmus thus presents certain special problems of comprehension and interpretation by virtue of his role or position in the schism, his message, and his personality. I do not intend to probe these factors in themselves any further. I have given my own brief statement and appraisal of them as background for what I shall now discuss. Controlling much of the opinion and controversy about Erasmus in his own day, they also bear on the subsequent judgment and evaluation of him. Let us now come down to more recent times and see how some modern historians have appraised the man.

Preserved Smith's biography of Erasmus to which I referred earlier is a good place to begin. First published in 1923, it was the fullest and most scholarly study of Erasmus published in America up to that time. It is still a very accessible book, having been reprinted as a paperback in 1962. Smith has given us a solid historical account of the great humanist's life, somewhat pedantic and a little archaic in its style, but substantial, full of detail, and not without present value. The Erasmus who emerges from his pages is essentially the champion of rational Christianity, an Erasmus "more skeptical and enlightened than most of his contemporaries."[9] It was not the scoffing rationalism that some have claimed, according to Smith, but one that struck out at the superstitious and credulous, saw religion as an ethical concern, and sought to rid it of its dogma. Indeed Erasmus' rational Christianity was primarily an undogmatic Christianity, and this, he declares, was one of the main reasons why Erasmus broke with Luther and the Protestants.[10] Reason and dogma it would seem were the great incompatibles, their tension the essence of Erasmus' story. Smith deplored the fact that Erasmus did not support the Reformation. "Convinced as I am that the Reformation was fundamentally a progressive movement," he wrote, "the culmination of the Renaissance, and above all the logical outcome of the teachings of Erasmus himself, I cannot but regard his later rejection of it as a mistake in itself and as a misfortune to the cause of liberalism."[11] Nevertheless Smith believed that Erasmus' efforts in "rationalizing religion" presaged and helped to prepare the enlightened future.[12] He was, in Smith's words, "the forerunner and exponent of that type of Christianity at present prevalent among large circles of our cultivated classes."

Smith's presentation of Erasmus as a rationalist heralding the Enlightenment and the Liberal Age is, or at least was, a common view. Derived from an earlier and cruder image of Erasmus as the Voltaire of the sixteenth century, it concentrated on his satiric thrusts at superstition and on his critical approach both as scholar and as observer of the human scene. It appears to have been a fairly characteristic nineteenth- and early-twentieth-century view, congenial to the more cultivated middle-class *Weltanschauung* of that era.[13] Nor is it entirely without its more recent versions. I am thinking chiefly of the thesis presented by H. A. Enno Van Gelder in *The Two Reformations in the Sixteenth Century* (The Hague, 1961).

Van Gelder sees Erasmus and the humanists inaugurating a more radical change in men's religious ideas than Luther and the Protestants. The latter still held to the traditional concept of Christianity as a doctrine of salvation, of man's redemption through Christ; the former shifted the whole emphasis, the whole orientation, to the moral or ethical sphere. For Erasmus, Van Gelder tells us, religion was "a doctrine of life instead of a mysterious redemption," and his view and mode of thinking are like that of the later rationalists.[14]

Such interpretations today have a rather old-fashioned ring. The product of less complicated times, they embody a perspective which not only is outmoded, but which rests on very dated cultural preconceptions. They tend to reduce Erasmus to the level of their own over-simplification. To some extent this is always inevitable, but in this instance it seems to be particularly unfortunate. There is so much more to Erasmus and his role in history than as a herald of rationalism or of ethical culture or as a precursor of the Enlightened Christianity that Smith saw about him. I was particularly struck in reading Smith, despite the factual detail, by the incompleteness and narrowness of the portrait he gives. The deeper aspects of Erasmus' religion are hardly grasped, Erasmus' concern with the Fathers and the influence of that rich patristic heritage are scarcely treated, and, most surprisingly, Erasmus' attitude and efforts toward conciliation and reunion in the face of schism are barely mentioned. In the light of this it is fair to say that the whole relationship of Erasmus to the Reformation is misconceived and that the place in history Smith accords him is one which needs radical correction and relocation.

The year after Smith's work appeared the famous biography of Erasmus by the Dutch scholar and professor of history at Leiden Johan Huizinga was published. His book, not so ponderous or documented as Smith's, is a more appealing study and is far more sophisticated and nuanced in its characterization. The Erasmus of Huizinga is not the champion of any great cause. He is the man of letters and the theologian. His work was significant, his influence extensive, and many of his qualities—gentleness, moderation—are admirable, but he is not one of history's heroes. "Erasmus is the man who is too sensible and moderate for the heroic."[15] Huizinga is particularly concerned with a personal analysis, and his chapters on Erasmus' mind and character are the heart of his book and its most interesting and controversial part.[16] The bent of Erasmus' mind was ethical and aesthetic, it sought freedom, clarity, simplicity, and it was acutely aware of the ambiguity of all things. But "the world of his mind is imaginary," Huizinga tells us. "Erasmus is never fully in contact with life."[17]

Nor is his character without its flaws: he tends to be self-centered, he is restless and discontent, he is not straightforward or decisive. These qualities in turn help to explain Erasmus' role in the schism. It is "extremely ambiguous."[18] He is not aware that his views are "no longer purely Catholic," and he fails too to understand the great issues and movements of his time.[19] This Erasmus, to whom Huizinga attributes a "velvet softness" and whom he calls a "recluse," certainly stands in sharp contrast to the portrait by Smith. Not his rationalism predominates, but his complex and withdrawn personality. Huizinga is one of the first to focus so intensively on the personality of the humanist reformer and to explain so much in terms of its qualities and deficiencies. He has not gone to the extreme of Erik Erikson in his psychoanalysis of the young Luther, but he has, I believe, exaggerated the personal equation as well as over-emphasized certain features of that personality itself. We could not give Erasmus too exalted a place in history on the strength of Huizinga's recommendation.

Another and quite different Erasmus appears in the pages of a study by the English scholar and writer Margaret Mann Phillips. Her book *Erasmus and the Northern Renaissance*, first published in 1949, is an exceedingly well wrought and sympathetic essay. Mrs. Phillips' Erasmus is the Christian humanist, the reformer, the man of sincerity and humor and "refreshing common sense." In the face of religious controversy and schism he is the apostle of "the Middle Way," faithful to his original ideals, seeking and continuing to seek a spiritual reform, but not the disruptive and intolerant reform of the Protestants.[20] This "middle way" for Mrs. Phillips is not a matter of weakness or indecision, as Huizinga and others would have it, but a genuine position, a valid and consistent program in tune with Erasmus' fundamental spirit. It is his glory and his heritage. She writes:

> That mellow, balanced sanity has always cast its spell, representing as it does the perfect work of the classical spirit tempered by the Christian ideal. It is indeed the middle way, not only between Catholic and Protestant, but between the mind and the heart. It needs on the one hand a liberated intellect, on the other a realization of the realms outside the reach of reason; a serene faith and a warm love of mankind are essentials to it. It is the climate of the mind in which humour grows, friendship blossoms and tolerance cultivates the flowers of the spirit: a tolerance resulting not from indolence but from decision and clear thinking.[21]

A third Erasmus thus arises—neither the champion of a rationalistic Christianity, nor the befuddled and indecisive spectator on life's drama, but the authentic Christian scholar and reformer pursuing a balanced middle course with clarity and consistency. A similar appraisal is given us in the biography published in 1969 by the noted American Reformation scholar Roland H. Bainton, a work well entitled *Erasmus of Christendom*. Bainton does not center his book, as Mrs. Phillips does, on the "middle way" theme, but he does present a moderate Erasmus, a man who cherished peace and concord, a man of piety and learning and deep religious purpose. The emphatic note struck by Bainton is the "inwardness" of Erasmus' religion. Erasmus sought above all to spiritualize religious life and practice—to turn it from the outward forms and ceremonials to an inward faith and dedication.[22] The spirit and the fruits of the spirit were what really mattered in the Christian dispensation.

In his preface Bainton tells us that Erasmus has not had his due on the score of interpretation. "Rejected by the Catholics as subversive and by the Protestants as evasive he has fallen chiefly into the hands of the rationalists who have appreciated him chiefly for his satire on contemporary superstitions."[23] Bainton intends to correct the image, and he does so, like Mrs. Phillips, by stressing the character and depth of Erasmus' religious thought and the seriousness of his Christian purpose. Though the work unfortunately is slightly flawed by a few annoying minor errors, Bainton's portrait, I believe, is more accurate than either Smith's or Huizinga's. There is, however, one aspect of Bainton's interpretation—and of Mrs. Phillips' too—on which I would like to comment. This is the explanation or view of Erasmus' relation to the Catholic Church. If for Smith Erasmus is actually a kind of liberal Protestant, for Bainton he is a liberal Catholic, indeed "the protagonist of liberal Catholic reform"[24] (in one place Bainton calls him "a precursor of the Counter-reformation"[25]). Yet the relationship between Erasmus and Catholicism, its authority, its tradition, its reform, is not well explored.[26] Bainton does not deny that Erasmus was and remained a Catholic, but the emphasis he places on Erasmus' spiritualizing tendencies and the conclusions he draws therefrom produce a Sacramentarian or Schwenkfeldian Erasmus who is not really Catholic at all. A line may run from Erasmus in that direction, as Bainton says, but the fact is that Erasmus stayed in the Church and apparently believed in it. I was left somewhat confused by this aspect of Bainton's otherwise very probing and enlightening study.

The question is a difficult one—Erasmus tends to elude conventional classification—but it is an important one, and it deserves very careful and discerning treatment. It is of considerable historical moment to know whether Erasmus' thought and spirituality and purpose were authentical-

Erasmus, by Hans Holbein, after 1523

The Metropolitan Museum of Art, Robert Lehman Collection, 1975

Folly speaks to her audience; Erasmus, with pointing finger, is to the left. By the Master of the Miracles of the Apostles, active in Leiden, ca. 1520–30.

Jean de Carondelet, by Jan Cornelisz Vermeyen, before 1525

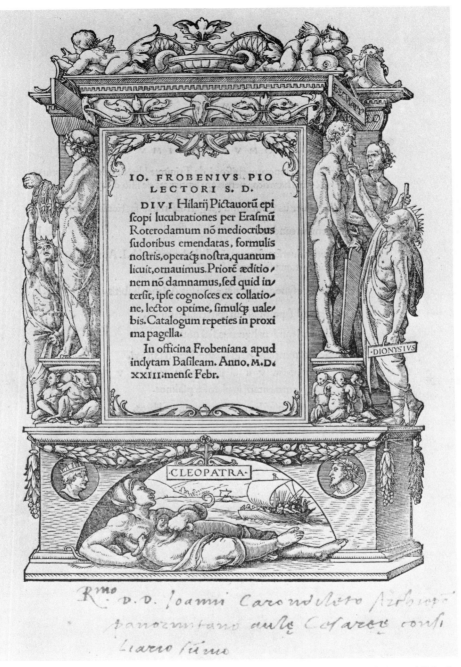

The title page of the presentation copy of Erasmus' edition of St. Hilary, published by Froben at Basel in 1523, and dedicated to Carondelet. With Erasmus' autograph inscription "To the Most Reverend lord, Lord Jean Carondelet, Archbishop of Palermo, chief counselor of the imperial court."

ly Catholic or not and to what extent they relate to tradition and to the needs of the then contemporary Church. The question, of course, has not exactly been neglected; but a good many of the analyses and appraisals of Erasmus on this score seem either vague and confusing, or even shallow and uninformed. I have never been able to understand, for example, what Huizinga means when he keeps insisting that Erasmus' creed and concept of the Church were "no longer purely Catholic."[27] I do understand what Joseph Lortz means when, judging Erasmus from a Catholic point of view, he characterizes Erasmus' thought as "cultural religiosity," but in that case I believe the description to be erroneous.[28] Mrs. Phillips' portrait of Erasmus with its emphasis on his "middle way" produces the tendency to locate Erasmus "between Catholic and Protestant." Perhaps this is meant to be understood loosely in the sense that Erasmus stood between two warring camps, but the designation is a bit misleading. She does not adequately clarify this crucial relationship.[29] Perhaps one cannot; or perhaps one cannot make the neat, decisive clarification I seem to demand. Perhaps Erasmus' spirituality and moderate position are actually in between. The suggestion of that in Mrs. Phillips' essay calls to mind the more extensive interpretation of the great French Erasmian scholar Augustin Renaudet, and her book reflects in this regard the view of the former professor at the Collège de France.

One of Renaudet's chief works is his *Etudes érasmiennes* (Paris, 1939). It is a very detailed study of Erasmus' writings and thought during the critical years at Basel from 1521 to 1529. Renaudet's dominant theme is what he calls Erasmus' *modernisme*. Borrowing a term which had been applied to a movement within the Catholic Church at the turn of the twentieth century—a movement which stressed the historical evolution and relativity of doctrine and which had been formally condemned by Rome in 1907—Renaudet applies it to Erasmus' Biblical humanism and religious thought.[30] It is a slightly prejudicial label, to say the least. He views Erasmus' Christianity as "a religion of pure spirit," undogmatic and ethical, breaking sharply with theological tradition and orthodox formulation. Ranaudet's approach associates him with the rationalist school of interpretation, but his appreciation and analysis of Erasmus' religion, it must be said, is both deeper and more sophisticated. A profounder Erasmus emerges from the pages of his careful study. He sees the so-called *modernisme* of Erasmus, however, as neither Protestant nor Catholic, as identifiable neither with the religion of Wittenberg and Zurich nor with that of Rome.[31] Erasmus is "between Roman conservatism and Lutheran revolution."[32] In a later book, *Erasme et l'Italie* (Geneva, 1954), Renaudet employed another memorable term to categorize Erasmus' position with respect to the rival Churches. The great humanist wanted, he tells us, a "troisième Eglise," a third Church.[33] This would be the Roman Church "profoundly reformed, renewed, modernized," but it is a Church which Renaudet by definition and explanation does not identify with the existing Catholic Church. It obviously is the ideal Church of Erasmian *modernisme*, though it is interesting to note that in *Erasme et l'Italie* Renaudet has replaced the latter designation by the term and concept of a "troisième Eglise."

In both instances, but particularly in support of his thesis that Erasmus sought a third Church, Renaudet makes use of a very interesting quotation from the humanist's *Hyperaspistes* of 1526.[34] Writing in response to Luther following the latter's attack on him in *De servo arbitrio*, Erasmus said: "I will bear with this Church [meaning the Catholic Church] until I see a better one." Renaudet interprets this as substantiating his general theme, and it becomes a text for introducing the Erasmus of the third Church, of the middle way. There are difficulties, however, in using the *Hyperaspistes* quotation in this way. Jean-Claude Margolin, for one, takes issue with the meaning Renaudet has drawn from it and indeed with Renaudet's whole interpretation in this area.

Margolin is a professor at Tours and the author of several recent studies in this field, in particular a general sketch or portrait of Erasmus, entitled *Erasme par lui-même* (Paris, 1965). Margolin gives us a scholarly, sensitive Erasmus whose Christianity is fully Catholic and whose religious thought embraces two fundamental principles: the spirit of liberty and the spirit of charity.[35] It is, Margolin tells us, "an immense commentary on the saying of St. Augustine: 'Love and do as you will'," and it is "perfectly orthodox, since it proceeds essentially from the Gospel."[36] His view of the *Hyperaspistes* quotation is that the full text does not permit Renaudet's interpretation.[37] In fact it actually affirms Erasmus' attachment or fidelity to the Catholic Church. It is prefaced by the clear statement "I have never defected from the Catholic Church," and the complete sentence so cherished by Renaudet reads: "I will bear with this Church until I see a better one, and it must bear with me until I become better." On the basis of the complete sentence, we might develop the thesis of a second Erasmus!

Margolin is at pains to insist that he seeks and attempts to describe the authentic Erasmus whose true face has too often been hidden by partisan interpretation and by the *quod erat demonstrandum* of those who have dealt with him. I share his attitude. Despite the real difficulties of understanding this complex personality and this incredibly prolific scholar and author, he has been wrenched too often by the one-sided perspectives and preconceived ideas of the historians who have portrayed him. He has continued to be in a sense the victim of polarization, of confessionalism, and of prejudice. The most serious distortion has been that of the rationalists who have been the least able to understand what he wrote and taught and sought to achieve. Nor have they been able even to start in that direction. It is almost inconceivable, for instance, that Preserved Smith should dismiss the great mass of his patristic work and scholarship and the integral role it had in his thought and program in a few pages in his chapter on Erasmus' "miscellaneous writings." Happily that situation has been and is being rectified, but, as Bainton has well pointed out, Erasmus in the past has not had his due.

The image, then, of a profoundly Christian Erasmus fully orthodox and Catholic has gradually emerged. On the basis of my own studies and judgment and frame of reference, it is the image of the great humanist reformer that I see as I try to understand his work and his role in the troubled age in which he lived. The view of Margolin, of course, is neither the first nor the only interpretation of Erasmus along this line. Two other contemporary French scholars have given us a comparable judgment based on an even more precise analysis of Erasmus' theological orientation. I refer to Louis Bouyer of the French Oratory and to Henri de Lubac, s.j., professor of theology at Lyons. Both men have written extensively, and their works which bear most fully in this instance on our theme are Bouyer's *Autour d'Erasme* (Paris, 1955), later translated and published here as *Erasmus and His Times*, and the fourth volume of de Lubac's magisterial *Exégèse médiévale* (Paris, 1964).[38] Both of these scholars insist on Erasmus' fidelity to the patristic tradition and they stress the significance of his scholarly endeavor to reform and renew theology through a return to Scripture and the Fathers. It was the foundation of his whole reform program, the main source of his spirituality and life's work. Both examine at some length the modernist or "third Church" thesis of Renaudet and reject it, and they view Erasmus' thought and purpose as being in perfect conformity with Catholic doctrine and Catholic tradition. He may stand in sharp contrast to the scholasticism of the late Middle Ages, but that in itself does not place him beyond the pale of orthodoxy or qualify his essential Catholic faith. In fact, as Catholic theologians themselves they hail the historic endeavor and achievement of Erasmus. Bouyer tells us that "his humanism reopened widely the permanent sources of Christian teaching" and that "this man who symbolizes better than anyone the renewal of the world ... performed at the same time the function of its Christian conscience."[39]

De Lubac, having considered the checkered course of Erasmus interpretation in the later part of his analysis, finally concludes with several texts from the letters of Thomas More defending and praising the noble work and virtue of his friend. "Nor surely can the faith of Erasmus be obscure," More wrote, "a faith adorned by so many labors, so many vigils, so many dangers, so many troubles, all sustained for the sake of Sacred Letters, the very storehouse of faith."[40]

This may be a suitable point at which to end our discussion of the problem and ways of interpreting Erasmus. We have returned at length to the judgment of a man who knew Erasmus intimately in his own time and who shared so many of his scholarly concerns, plans, and ideals. More's appraisal at least must be given great weight, and it points in a direction quite different from that taken by many later interpreters of Erasmus and his role, though not from that of some of the more recent and more perceptive ones.

In the above essay I have indicated that if we wished we could continue our survey of historians who have dealt with Erasmus. It now strikes me as imperative that we do so. The reason is the appearance in a recent issue of *The American Historical Review* of a psychoanalytic study of the humanist, entitled "The Character of Erasmus."[41] It is a collaborative work by an historian at The Catholic University of America, Nelson H. Minnich, and a Jesuit psychiatrist, W. W. Meissner, M.D. The two authors purport to give a coherent psychological portrait—"a psychoanalytically intelligible configuration consistent with the historical data"—of their subject. Following through on the picture Johan Huizinga presented in the middle chapters of his biography more than fifty years ago they have more clinically examined Erasmus' behavior and have more narrowly and even more negatively viewed his troubled state. Their psychiatric concentration and critical forthrightness are unrelieved by any of the literary grace or balance or fullness of context that made Huizinga's study a notable work.

The Minnich–Meissner excursion into psychohistory amounts to a case study of a well-known but severely disturbed personality. The authors see Erasmus as latently homosexual, seriously narcissistic, and generally paranoid, and they causally relate these pathological aspects of his character to the circumstances of his birth and early childhood—that is, to his illegitimacy and especially to his being rejected and abandoned by his father. There is a paragraph toward the end of their article which sums up the main theme of their interpretation, though it does not by any means embrace all the "dark elements" these two probers have observed in the character of Erasmus:

> Erasmus lived under what Gregory Rochlin calls "the tyranny of narcissism." His life appears to have been an incessant seeking for recognition, acceptance, and adulation from his fellow man. Questioning or criticism of his motives or performance could prompt in him an anxious and threatened response which mobilized his resources and rushed them to the defense of his embattled narcissism. Erasmus' sense of self-worth and self-esteem was continually in jeopardy and required constant reinforcement. His feelings of inadequacy were reflected in his depression, disillusionment, skepticism, and isolation. Much of his Herculean literary labor can be seen as a gigantic effort to redeem some sense of inner value, as though he sought to build an outer façade of accomplishment and sophistication to conceal a self-perception of worthlessness and vileness.

The last sentence in particular is interesting as an explanation of Erasmus' career and life's work, and a few pages previously the authors expressed this same view with even less qualification (though the phrase "in a sense" may be intended as a qualifier). "The whole corpus of Erasmian writings," they declared, "was, in a sense, an elaborate self-justification."

This unflattering image of one of Europe's most famous and most productive scholars is based on information gleaned from his *Compendium vitae* and from some of his letters and a few writings (*The Praise of Folly* looms large, although the authors call it "uncharacteristic"), or rather it is based on inferences and impressions derived therefrom and from Erasmus' behavior in general. It is a "clinical interpretation," and the authors frankly acknowledge that they have not restricted themselves to a cautious historical investigation but have sought "a clear and coherent psychoanalytic interpretation." The aim and the methodology in this instance seem risky, to say the least, and if a lay historian may venture to comment on the actual analysis (the authors do not appear too disposed to this), the grounds for the interpretation are insufficient and the interpretation itself is highly tendentious. Despite the considerable amount of footnoting one senses an inadequate acquaintance with the Erasmian corpus, and one perceives an acceptance of the view of Erasmus, or a part of the view, which some latter-day historians, notably Huizinga and John Joseph Mangan, have given us. Thus to one fairly familiar with the writings and work of Erasmus and with the historiographical traditions of interpreting him the Minnich–Meissner presentation lacks the authority which for some its psychoanalytic approach and terminology might bestow upon it.

And how to judge this "clinical interpretation" if not on the basis of the historical evidence? The historian is naturally reluctant to turn over his profession to the psychiatrist or accept his experience as a higher revelation. This does not mean that the historian refuses to make use of other skills or insights, but it means that his understanding rests primarily on his conscientious and informed examination of the evidence. Many of the pronouncements in the article at hand will certainly strengthen his fidelity to his craft. For example, to speak of Erasmus' literary and scholarly labors —that is, his life's work—as a huge effort to justify himself and overcome an "injured narcissism" is absurd or at best an exceedingly narrow and irrelevant "clinical" observation. One need only to study the *Adagia* which contains so many marvelous essays and which had so many enlargements and editions in Erasmus' lifetime, or to examine the great edition of St. Jerome over which Erasmus labored with such devotion and dedication and which includes among other things the first critical biography of the saint, to realize how misplaced and inaccurate and indeed unworthy the judgment is.

There are several other features of the Minnich–Meissner analysis to which one might also take exception, such as their understanding of *The Praise of Folly*, their view of Erasmus' friendship with Thomas More, and their notion (similar to Huizinga's) of Erasmus' indecision and ambivalence. I have given my own explanation of *The Praise of Folly*, admittedly a controversial work, elsewhere in this volume. I suggest that the view of More as a "major father figure" for Erasmus is jargonized nonsense and damaging to any appreciation of the substantial bond of friendship which did exist between the two humanists. The charge of indecision and ambivalence has to be considered in the full context of Erasmus' goals and labors. Erasmus did have clear aims, firm convictions, and high ideals, and he held to them with remarkable constancy throughout his life. While we are criticizing specific points in the article I should also like to comment on the curious "speculation" of the authors (pages 604–6) regarding Erasmus' attraction to humanism and aversion to scholasticism. They indicate that humanism satisfied certain needs of his disturbed personality and "allowed him to escape his origins, avoid entangling loyalties, and sink few roots" (why John O'Malley's article on Erasmus and Luther in *The Sixteenth Century Journal*, 5 [1974] is footnoted at this point is puzzling), whereas he found scholasticism "too difficult" and thus an affront to his self-esteem. Undoubtedly personal inclinations and motives play a role in our intellectual choices, but to personalize Erasmus' "decision" on this important issue to such an extent is a gross and misleading exaggeration. Humanism had its own inherent appeal and was beginning to sweep Europe in the latter part of the fifteenth century. Many other scholars besides Erasmus were won enthusiastically to the cause, and we may suppose that broad cultural factors as well as specific historical circumstances were operative. Also, the emphasis on the "difficulty" of scholastic studies is a novel and unexpected note to strike in explaining Erasmus' attitude. That attitude had deeper and firmer footing, just as his frequent criticism of scholastic theology had a serious reform purpose. Anthony Levi's introduction in the Penguin *Praise of Folly*, to which the authors refer (as well as the article by Father O'Malley we mentioned above), should have made that clear.

The problem with analyses such as this is not simply that they are inadequately grounded and narrowly conceived but that they drain a person's aims and efforts and life itself of any real meaning. What we carry away from the article is that Erasmus was a pathetically troubled and sick individual whose "character" was damaged at the outset by his rejection by his father. The picture is unworthy of so great a man, and what is more it is untrue. Indeed it smacks of the kind of attack which rival scholastic theologians launched against him in his own day, save that a Freudian garb now cloaks the rancor and dismay of his adversaries. The correspondence between old and new critics may be closer than one thinks, for in both cases a rigid methodology, an arcane terminology, and a concern with what proves to be irrelevant tend to prevail. The Freudians, it would appear, have grasped the cudgels from the faltering hands of the late medieval scholastics. Not every psychologist or psychiatrist, however, would arrive at the same diagnosis of Erasmus. I recall seeing a film of Carl Jung a few years ago on television. He was being interviewed in his study, and on the wall in back of where he sat there hung a reproduction of Holbein's great portrait of Erasmus at the Louvre. That was not an accidental display, and I am certain Jung had a very different opinion of the famous scholar and Christian humanist than the authors of the analysis we have been considering.

Finally I should like to note a brief appreciation of Erasmus which I read in Chapter VII of Rudolf Pfeiffer's excellent *History of Classical Scholarship from 1300 to 1850* (Oxford, 1976) about the same time that I read the Minnich–Meissner article. It served fortuitously as what Erasmus would call an *antidotum* and refocused my attention on his actual labors and contribution. Pfeiffer concluded his short account with these words:

Erasmus used his scholarship and humanism for the promotion of the universal Church, that it might retain the spiritual leadership of the whole of Christendom which the Church of his day was in danger of losing. . . . He did not fail, as is so often said, especially by historians; the others failed to accept his warning. And what we may call the tragedy in Erasmus' life lies in the fact that he was to a large extent misunderstood by the Church, to which he had devoted all the vigour of his versatile mind.

Interpreting Erasmus continues to be a difficult and controversial task, but like Thomas More, Pfeiffer understands his subject and gives us the right judgment on which to end.

NOTES

1. CHR, pp. 29–30.

2. Jean Rouschausse, *Erasmus and Fisher, Their Correspondence, 1511–1524* (Paris, 1968), p. 83. See also Margaret Mann Phillips, "Some Last Words of Erasmus," in *Luther, Erasmus and the Reformation*, edd. John C. Olin, James D. Smart, and Robert E. McNally, s.j. (New York, 1969), pp. 90–91, for further comment on this predicament.

3. This is amply covered in one fashion or another in practically every volume on Erasmus. For a good review of Erasmus' relations with Luther and Lutheranism, see C. R. Thompson's introduction to his edition of Erasmus' *Inquisitio de fide* (New Haven, 1950).

4. CHR, p. 17 n. 36, and Martin Luther, *The Bondage of the Will*, trans. J. I. Packer and O. R. Johnston (London, 1957), pp. 74, et passim.

5. Phillips, op. cit., p. 97.

6. Augustin Renaudet, *Erasme et l'Italie* (Geneva, 1954), p. 150.

7. Marcel Bataillon, *Erasme et l'Espagne* (Paris, 1937), p. 760.

8. Rouschausse, loc. cit.

9. Preserved Smith, *Erasmus, a Study of His Life, Ideals and Place in History* (repr. ed.; New York, 1962), Preface, pp. 159, 323, 441, et passim.

10. *Ibid.*, pp. 324–25.

11. *Ibid.*, p. 439.

12. *Ibid.*, Preface and p. 159.

13. Bruce E. Mansfield, "Erasmus in the Nineteenth Century: The Liberal Tradition," *Studies in the Renaissance*, 15 (1968), 193–219.

14. H. A. Enno Van Gelder, *The Two Reformations in the Sixteenth Century* (The Hague, 1961), pp. 143–44.

15. Johan Huizinga, *Erasmus of Rotterdam*, trans. F. Hopman (New York, 1952), p. 188.

16. I.e., Chaps. XII–XIV.

17. *Ibid.*, pp. 115–16.

18. *Ibid.*, p. 142.

19. *Ibid.*, p. 136.

20. Margaret Mann Phillips, *Erasmus and the Northern Renaissance* (London, 1949), Chap. VI.

21. *Ibid.*, pp. 223–24.

22. Roland H. Bainton, *Erasmus of Christendom* (New York, 1969), pp. 67–68, et passim.

23. *Ibid.*, p. vii.

24. *Ibid.*, p. 35.

25. *Ibid.*, p. 193.

26. *Ibid.*, pp. 193–96, for example.

27. Huizinga, op. cit., pp. 102, 136, 168.

28. Joseph Lortz, *How the Reformation Came*, trans. Otto M. Knab (New York, 1964), pp. 80–88.

29. See also Mrs. Phillips, "Some Last Words of Erasmus" for some later comment and analysis of this relationship.

30. Augustin Renaudet, *Etudes érasmiennes* (Paris, 1939), Introduction and Chap. IV.

31. *Ibid.*, pp. xxi–xxii.

32. *Ibid.*, p. 122.

33. Renaudet, *Erasme et l'Italie*, pp. xi, 175, 200ff.

34. Renaudet, *Etudes érasmiennes*, pp. xxi and 260, and *idem*, *Erasme et l'Italie*, pp. 9, 175, 200, 247.

35. J.-C. Margolin, *Erasme par lui-même* (Paris, 1965), pp. 69–85.

36. *Ibid.*, pp. 76 and 81.

37. *Ibid.*, pp. 84–85. Henri de Lubac, s.j., *Exégèse médiévale*, Second Part, II (Paris, 1964), 468–70, and Myron P. Gilmore, *Humanists and Jurists* (Cambridge, Mass., 1963), p. 133, share Margolin's view.

38. The section on Erasmus in de Lubac's *Exégèse médiévale*, Second Part, II, is on pp. 427–82. For a further statement by Bouyer see his "Erasmus in Relation to the Medieval Biblical Tradition," in *The Cambridge History of the Bible*, II, ed. G. W. H. Lampe (Cambridge, 1969), 492–505.

39. Louis Bouyer, *Erasmus and His Times*, trans. F. X. Murphy (Westminster, Md., 1959), pp. 149–50.

40. Quoted in de Lubac, op. cit., Second Part, II, 479.

41. Vol. 83, No. 3 (June 1978), 598–624.

6

ERASMUS AND ST. IGNATIUS LOYOLA

THE POSSIBILITY that St. Ignatius Loyola, founder of the Society of Jesus and perhaps the most pre-eminent figure of the Counter Reformation, was influenced by Erasmus and the broad current of reform humanism that swept Europe in the early sixteenth century is an interesting and attractive speculation. It has the merit, if any substance can be found in it, of overthrowing certain stereotypes and of casting fresh light on the nature of Catholic reform and on the interplay of ideas in this age of religious crisis. Even as a subject for inquiry it can lead to a new investigation and a new appraisal of several important aspects of Ignatius' life and thought. In view of the tendency to consider the Spanish saint in a manner quite routine and fraught with preconception, this will be no small service.

But what in the first place could give rise to the thought that there is a link between Ignatius and Erasmus? Neither personal encounter, nor literary reference, nor obvious similarity of character or mission suggests a connection. In fact at first glance they present a rather sharp and inimical contrast, and the disciplined, orthodox, and obedient spirit of the one seems almost the antithesis of the critical and undogmatic spirit of the other. And what specific mention one may find of Erasmus and his works in the sources relating to Ignatius indicate an aversion on his part toward the great humanist. Since Erasmus died in 1536, before the name or importance of Ignatius could have come to his attention, there is, of course, no reference to the saint in his extensive correspondence and literary work. Where, then, lies a relationship positive or meaningful enough to warrant the historian's consideration?

The answer to this may simply be that the historian, seeking to understand more fully the pattern of religious events in this age, pursues this theme for what it may be worth. His own orientation, his own interests, and perhaps some vague intimation of a bond may have suggested the question as a fruitful hypothesis.[1] Whatever the point of departure may

---

An earlier version of this essay appeared in *Luther, Erasmus, and the Reformation*, edd. John C. Olin, James D. Smart, and Robert E. McNally, s.j. (New York: Fordham University Press, 1969), pp. 114–33.

have been, however, he would soon confront the fact that Ignatius read, or at least began to read, Erasmus' *Enchiridion militis christiani* in his early days as a student. With this golden nugget his exploration would begin. And at this point too our story may pass from the mere posing of the problem to the scrutiny of the circumstances and the evidence that seem relevant.

As is well known, Ignatius undertook serious academic work rather late in life. If his birth be placed in 1491, it was not until his thirty-third year in 1524 that he began Latin instruction in Barcelona and the long and checkered course of study that led eventually to a Paris master of arts in 1534.[2] What preceded these student years was his life as a Spanish caballero and soldier and then, following a great conversion, the months of penitence, prayer, and pilgrimage that inaugurate his religious career. The conversion took place during his recuperation from a battle wound he received in the spring of 1521, fighting against the French at Pamplona in Navarre. Reading of Christ and His saints, he resolved to serve our Lord and do great deeds, like the saints, out of love of God. This initially found expression in the desire to go to Jerusalem, and in early 1522 he set out from his native Guipúzcoa on his pilgrim's way. His journey took him first to the shrine of our Lady at Montserrat in Catalonia and thence to nearby Manresa where he remained for several months. He underwent there a deep religious experience, received, in his own words, "a great illumination in his understanding," and completed the transformation that his convalescent reading had begun.[3] At the beginning of 1523 he left Barcelona for Rome and Jerusalem. To his great joy he reached his destination, but the Franciscan guardians of the Holy Places rejected his plea to remain among them, and reluctantly he returned to Spain. It was now—in early 1524—"inclined to study so as to be able to help souls," as he expressed it, that he began his education in Barcelona.[4]

From there Ignatius passed to Alcalá in 1526, where he attended lectures in philosophy at the university which the great Cardinal of Spain, Ximenes de Cisneros, had founded fewer than twenty years before. Suspected of being an *alumbrado*, however, he had serious trouble with the Inquisition and was investigated and confined. Finally to escape the restraints that had been placed upon him he went to Salamanca, but there too he aroused suspicion, and further trial and imprisonment were his fate. He then made up his mind to go to Paris in order to work more freely in helping souls and to study more effectively to this end. He arrived in Paris in February 1528, and there he remained until the spring of 1535. Such is the briefest outline of Ignatius' early years, his pilgrim years. I should now like to speak about several incidents during this time that bear upon our theme.

As I have already said, Ignatius at the outset of his studies read Erasmus' *Enchiridion*. The story is told by Pedro Ribadeneira, Ignatius' first biographer, a member of the young Society of Jesus and a man who knew the saint intimately in his later years.[5] Ribadeneira places the event in Barcelona when Ignatius was studying there in 1524-25 and tells us that Ignatius undertook the reading at the suggestion of some pious and learned men, including his confessor. As he did, however, Ribadeneira reports, the saint "observed that the reading of that book chilled the spirit of God in him and gradually extinguished the ardor of devotion." Finally he cast the book aside, and he conceived such an aversion for the author that he never afterward would read him, nor would he permit his works to be read in the Society.

This account in Ribadeneira is the most extended reference in the Ignatian sources to Erasmus. In fact, it is almost the only one—or more precisely, it is the most basic and comprehensive one, and what other references there are stand in close relationship to it. We shall refer to these as we proceed. At any rate the Ribadeneira text has given posterity the general picture of an Ignatius hostile to Erasmus and his spirit from the start, and from it, as from a well, is drawn the usual interpretation of their antithesis. Other factors indeed may be brought into play to explain their divergence, but Ribadeneira's account is fundamental and controlling.[6]

There are, however, certain critical observations that may be made about this key text and certain difficulties in accepting it at face value. This is said in view of a number of circumstances which we shall now discuss, but the one general critique that may be launched against this account is that Ribadeneira is describing essentially a very personal experience at second hand more than forty years after the event itself and that his description would seem to be a faulty and inaccurate ex-post-facto reconstruction. The lack of any really adequate corroboration for this particular story he tells makes him all the more vulnerable to the critic's knife.

For one thing, there is the problem whether Ignatius actually read the *Enchiridion* at Barcelona or a short time later after he came to Alcalá. The question is quite important, and it arises in the first place because there is a brief entry in the Memorial or diary of González de Cámara, an assistant and secretary of Ignatius' in Rome, for February 28, 1555, to the effect that when Ignatius was a student at Alcalá he was advised by many, including his confessor, to read Erasmus' work, but that having heard there were "differences and doubts about the author" he did not want to do so.[7] González' statement has led some, including Marcel Bataillon and

Paul Dudon, to believe that Ribadeneira erred in placing the incident he describes in Barcelona rather than in Alcalá, and for several reasons I am inclined to agree.[8] First, the state of Ignatius' Latin at Barcelona in these early years would have made reading the *Enchiridion* a very difficult, if not impossible, operation. We know from his autobiography that when he came to Paris in 1528 he had to begin his study of Latin grammar all over again, so shaky were his foundations.[9] Second, a Castilian version of Erasmus' treatise, artfully translated by a canon of Palencia, was published at Alcalá in 1526, the year Ignatius came to that university city, and he certainly would have had access to this edition.[10] In fact, he had more than simple access. He knew the printer, Miguel de Eguía, and his brother Diego, who, as Ignatius himself tells us, "helped him with their alms to support the poor, and maintained three [of his] companions in their house."[11] Miguel subsequently published several other works of Erasmus', including the *De libero arbitrio*, and in 1540 his brothers Diego and Esteban joined Ignatius in Rome to become members of the new Society. The concrete situation here revealed would certainly seem to link Ignatius quite closely with the vigorous Erasmian movement at Alcalá. This possibility is heightened by the fact that Ignatius' confessor at Alcalá was a Portuguese priest by the name of Manual Miona, himself an Erasmian and disciple of Bernardino Tovar who along with his brother Juan Vergara was a friend of Erasmus'.[12] Indeed it seems very probable that the confessor Ribadeneira tells us urged Ignatius to read the *Enchiridion* was Miona, and, if this be allowed, then Alcalá becomes the place of the reading. And if Ignatius read the Spanish edition of the *Enchiridion* at Alcalá, then he was introduced to Erasmus under conditions that are extremely interesting and suggestive. In short, the strong likelihood that it was Alcalá begins to raise some fairly serious doubts about the whole tenor of Ribadeneira's account. And further evidence, I believe, only accentuates the suspicion.

My second observation about the Ribadeneira text concerns his description of Ignatius' reaction to the *Enchiridion*—it "chilled the spirit of God in him and gradually extinguished the ardor of devotion." I submit that the reading of the *Enchiridion*, and especially of its opening chapters and especially in the beautiful Castilian version, *suavizada y mitigada*, could not have had the effect on Ignatius that Ribadeneira describes.[13] This is not to say that the saint would have warmed to it as he did to the *Imitation of Christ* which had very deep and enduring influence on his life,[14] but that he would not have found anything really offensive in it and indeed may have found much that was meaningful and applicable to him. The fact that it was addressed to a courtier and soldier, a caballero, who wished to change his life, the fact that Erasmus used a military analogy and urged his reader to campaign as a soldier of Christ under the standard of Christ, the striking and lengthy reference to water "as a symbol of knowledge of God's law," which immediately recalls Ignatius' own account of his "illumination" at the river near Manresa[15]—all this in the very first pages of the *Enchiridion* could hardly have failed to impress the pilgrim student.

There is also a passage toward the middle of the *Enchiridion* that deserves special attention in terms of a possible influence on Ignatius. The correspondence between it and a major statement of the saint is so close that there are grounds for believing that Ignatius may have borrowed from it.[16] I refer to the fourth rule which Erasmus presents as a guide to the Christian life—the rule that Christ is our only goal and that we must subordinate and direct everything to attain this goal.[17] In thought and in phrasing it is remarkably similar to the Principle and Foundation of the *Spiritual Exercises*, itself the classic statement of Ignatius' great rule of indifference or subordination.[18] Erasmus declares that whatever you encounter as you press toward your goal, "that you must reject or accept solely to the extent that it hinders or helps your journey," and he states that some things, such as health, learning, and the like, are neutral and that "of this last category, therefore, one should pursue none for its own sake, nor should he rely upon them any more or less than they help him to hit the final mark." Ignatius' Principle and Foundation reads as follows:

> Man is created to praise, reverence, and serve God our Lord, and by this means to save his soul. All other things on the face of the earth are created for man to help him fulfill the end for which he is created. From this it follows that man is to use these things to the extent that they will help him to attain his end. Likewise, he must rid himself of them in so far as they prevent him from attaining it. Therefore we must make ourselves indifferent to all created things, in so far as it is left to the choice of our free will and is not forbidden. Acting accordingly, for our part, we should not prefer health to sickness, riches to poverty, honor to dishonor, a long life to a short one, and so in all things we should desire and choose only those things which will best help us attain the end for which we are created.

Whatever conclusion one may draw from this striking resemblance, one can at least question Ribadeneira's text on the basis of it, and aver that Ignatius and Erasmus shared a very fundamental attitude and expressed it in a very similar mode.[19] Rule four of the *Enchiridion* could not have "chilled the spirit of God" in the saint. The more likely conjecture is that it contributed to the formulation of his own thought in the *Spiritual Exercises*.

With reference to Ignatius and the *Enchiridion* Marcel Bataillon has another interesting relationship to suggest. He advances the notion that Ignatius' concept of a religious order reflects the dictum *Monachatus non est pietas* found in the last pages of the *Enchiridion*, and thus he associates the organization and character of the Society of Jesus with Erasmus' criticism of the prevailing pattern of monastic life.[20] His argument rests chiefly on the fact that Ignatius suppressed choir or the chanting of the divine office in the new Society and that this bold step was viewed as a serious and even scandalous break with long tradition.[21] Many other features of the Society of Jesus, I believe, can also be assimiliated into the Bataillon thesis—its emphasis on education and learning,[22] the long period of testing and preparation before solemn profession,[23] the mitigation of traditional monastic practices regarding fasting and other penances, its indifference concerning a distinctive garb,[24] the very name it assumed. Ignatius may not have been consciously inspired by the *Enchiridion* or any other specific work of Erasmus when he and his companions planned and organized their Society in Rome in 1539, but the fact remains that he did found a new and different order and that in a good many respects it does take into account the criticisms of Erasmus and others of the friars and the monks. In terms of his own vocation and spirituality he is saying something quite similar to the dictum *Monachatus non est pietas*. This may be one of the chief reasons why men like the Venetian humanist Cardinal Gasparo Contarini championed the new foundation and others like the anti-Erasmian Dominican theologian Melchor Cano vigorously opposed it.

To return once more to the Ribadeneira text, there is a third comment I should like to make in criticism of it. Ribadeneira tells us that Ignatius conceived such an aversion when he read the *Enchiridion* that he would not permit Erasmus' books to be read in the Society—*et passim in Societate nostra legi vetuerit*. This is simply not the case. Ignatius never enjoined such a prohibition. Erasmus was read in the Jesuit colleges and presumably by the members of the Society. The clearest indication of this is in a letter written by Father Annibal du Coudray to Juan Polanco, Ignatius' secretary, in Rome in July 1551.[25] Father du Coudray describes the program of studies at the Jesuit college in Messina, a college Ignatius commissioned Jerome Nadal to establish in 1548. Like other Jesuit colleges, it was a trilingual college, and its curriculum is very important for providing a model or base for other colleges, including the Roman college, and for the later *Ratio studiorum*.[26] Du Coudray tells us that Erasmus' *De copia verborum* and his *De conscribendis epistolis* are used in the humanities class.[27] This testimony does not allow us to accept Ribadeneira's account.

After 1552, however, there are certain references in the letters and in-
structions of Ignatius which do indicate that he was uneasy about the use
of Erasmus' books in the colleges and that he would like to see them
replaced by others.[28] In 1553 Polanco wrote to du Coudray in words to that
effect, but he assured him that the present policy at Messina of using Erasmus was not objectionable and that they could continue to do so.[29] Finally
it appears that in 1555 Nadal visited certain Jesuit communities, inspected
their libraries, and set apart the works of Erasmus, Vives, and some other
authors until Ignatius came to a decision about them.[30] From all this
evidence we can only conclude that the Society did read and use Erasmus
in their schools and that Ignatius up to the last year of his life permitted
it, though in his later years—after 1552—he grew quite concerned about
the problem. Ignatius' concern and caution, I submit, is reflective of a general attitude toward Erasmus that began to harden in these years and of a
climate of opinion that was superorthodox, suspicious, and unbending.[31]
Prudence became his guide in this matter, for he had no desire to see his
Society falter under the burden of Erasmus and other controversial authors.[32] It had, indeed, enough problems of its own. There are no grounds,
as far as I can see, for connecting this cautionary attitude with a reading
of the *Enchiridion* almost thirty years before.[33]

It will be clear by now that I am extremely skeptical of the story Ribadeneira tells. I must confess that I see it as embodying an attitude toward
Erasmus and a handling of the delicate problem of Ignatius and Erasmus
more in keeping with the anti-Erasmian spirit of the Counter Reformation
—that is, of the time in which it was written—than with the actual facts
of the case. The same prudence that may have guided Ignatius in his last
years with respect to the use of Erasmus' works by the Society may also
have dictated the inaccurate and unlikely story Ribadeneira relates. The
fact that he concludes with a reference to the prohibition of Erasmus'
books in the Society, erroneous though it is, would seem to bear this out.
The Society had to disengage from any overt Erasmianism, and one might
say that its founder had to be placed in the other camp.[34]

There are, however, other reasons for rejecting the image of an Ignatius
hostile to Erasmus and his spirit from the start, and for calling into question the interpretation so general in Jesuit historiography of an antithesis
between the two men. Thus at long last we may take leave of that basic
text in Ribadeneira which we have been analyzing and proceed to certain
other events and episodes in Ignatius' life which suggest a degree of affinity
with Erasmus and the movement he represents. I mean that I intend not
to make Ignatius an Erasmian in the usual sense of that term, but simply

to show that a "wall of separation" did not exist between them. In the absence of that wall lies the possibility of a meaningful interchange.

When Ignatius, because of the trouble and interference which marked the course of his studies and lay apostolate, left Spain and came to Paris in early 1528, he first entered the College of Montaigu. There as an extern he renewed his study of Latin grammar. Montaigu was one of the more than fifty colleges which the University of Paris comprised, and its history in this period is famous. It had been reformed by the austere John Standonck in whose hard days Erasmus had the misfortune (as he saw it) of enrolling there, it was attended by the young John Calvin who left with his degree on the eve of Ignatius' entry, and, more to our point, it was associated in the 1520s with the rigid scholasticism and anti-humanism of its former principal, Noël Béda, one of Erasmus' most vigorous and intransigent enemies. Béda, then syndic of the faculty of theology at Paris, but still "master of the house" at Montaigu, was in the very midst of the campaign he had mounted against Erasmus and the French humanist Jacques Lefèvre when Ignatius arrived.[35] These scholars had been censured by the Sorbonne and denounced as clandestine Lutherans, and the reform humanism they represented was viewed with the gravest suspicion and alarm by many of Paris' foremost theologians. Béda was at their head. It would be remarkable if the attention of Ignatius at Montaigu was not soon drawn to the issues and the personalities involved. What were his views? Where did his sympathies lie? Unfortunately the record is silent, at least insofar as any explicit judgment is expressed. But there are, I think, very clear indications that Ignatius cannot be ranged on the side of Béda and the anti-humanists.

In the first place he left Montaigu after his Latin studies were completed and in the fall of 1529 entered the rival college of Sainte-Barbe for the philosophy courses which would lead eventually to his master of arts. The shift is interesting, for Sainte-Barbe was a more liberal college than the one he left and was quite penetrated by the new humanism which Béda so deplored. Its principal was a Portuguese, Diego de Gouvea, a Sorbonne theologian with an outlook very comparable to Béda's, but he was frequently engaged in diplomatic tasks for the Portuguese king, and the direction of his college during Ignatius' time was in the hands of his nephew, André de Gouvea, a man thoroughly sympathetic to humanist ideas.[36] There the Spanish humanist Juan Gelida taught, and there Nicolas Cop, whose inaugural address as rector of the university on All Saints' Day in 1533 stirred such excitement, was appointed regent by André in 1531. The college was decidedly more *aéré et ouvert* than the halls of

Montaigu.[37] Whether this played any part in Ignatius' decision to move to Sainte-Barbe is hard to know, but two inferences, I think, can be drawn: (1) Ignatius evidently had no powerful attachment to the school of Béda,[38] and (2) he did not scorn the livelier intellectual atmosphere of Sainte-Barbe. From quite another standpoint it was a most fortunate decision. Living at the college, Ignatius was to share a room with two young students who had entered Sainte-Barbe a few years before he did. Their names were henceforth to be joined with his in the great enterprise that awaited them. They were a young nobleman from Navarre, Francis Xavier, and a young man of peasant stock from Savoy, Peter Faber.

Another incident that may well be indicative of Ignatius' attitude in these Paris years is a visit he paid to the famous Spanish humanist Juan Luis Vives in Bruges probably in the summer of 1529. Ignatius after he came to Paris made several trips to Flanders to beg his support from well-to-do Spanish merchants there. On one of these excursions he was invited to dinner by Vives who had returned to Bruges from England and his court post in 1528. Juan Polanco in his life of Ignatius gives us the account of their meeting and of a discussion they had on the subject of the Lenten fast.[39] Ignatius took exception to the views of Vives and argued with him, according to Polanco, and the biographer continues that Ignatius "began to have doubts about the spirit that moved him, and subsequently forbade the reading of his books in our Society, even those that contained nothing objectionable, in the same way as he forbade the reading of Erasmus." This account, however, as James Brodrick points out, "is not entirely satisfactory."[40] There are three reasons for such an appraisal: (1) because of classes in Paris it is most unlikely that Ignatius visited Bruges during Lent, as Polanco states; (2) it is hard to believe that Ignatius, a guest in the home of the learned and gentle Vives, would have argued the way Polanco describes or have come away with the harsh impression Polanco attributes to him; (3) Ignatius did not subsequently forbid the reading of Vives in the Society. The situation with regard to that problem is the same as in the case of Erasmus, with whose name Vives is generally linked in the references to his books. On the other hand, Father Dudon, reconstructing this interesting encounter at Bruges, depicts the meeting of the two great Spaniards as the occasion for a very pleasant and stimulating conversation.[41] All the circumstances, apart from the Counter Reformation moralizing of Polanco, lead one to agree. I submit therefore that the dinner party at Vives' home reveals Ignatius as not being hostile to the humanist movement, and I raise the point that it possibly—just possibly—may have had some bearing on Ignatius' decision to shift to

Sainte-Barbe. Vives himself had once been a student at Paris, and he had come to reject with vehemence the scholastic dialectics that had such a citadel there.[42] It would not be surprising that he advised Ignatius to leave Montaigu and enter the more open and enlightened precincts of Sainte-Barbe.[43]

So favorable an interpretation of Ignatius' meeting with Vives is perhaps corroborated by this very interesting and significant fact: namely, that the oldest extant copy of the *Spiritual Exercises* is in the hand of an English disciple of Vives, a priest by the name of John Helyar.[44] Helyar had studied under Vives at Corpus Christi College, Oxford. He later became rector of Warblington, the parish church of the Pole family.[45] He knew and wrote in praise of Erasmus. In 1534 he left England for religious reasons and came to the continent, where sometime within the next few years, probably at Paris, he took the *Spiritual Exercises* under the direction either of Ignatius or of Peter Faber. His manuscript dates from this time.

Helyar's document must certainly be considered a link between Ignatius on the one hand and Vives, Erasmus, and Reginald Pole on the other. It may also indicate, as Bataillon suggests, a kinship between Erasmian spirituality and the Ignatian approach to piety and prayer.[46] In this instance the meditations on the life and passion of Christ, which so major a part of the *Spiritual Exercises* comprises, would undoubtedly have struck a responsive chord in Helyar. Indeed the whole moral and Christocentric spirit of Ignatius' discipline, as well as its fundamental interiority, would make, it seems to me, a strong appeal to the devout humanist. Here was a method, a way of personal reform, quite different from the external practices and the accessory devotions the humanists so frequently deplored. But regardless of how we may note the points of resemblance between the two spiritualities, the very existence of Helyar's manuscript affords concrete evidence of a certain compatibility. The spirit of Ignatius is not the antithesis of the spirit of Vives and Erasmus.

There is one last piece of evidence I would present at this time which casts light on the relationship we are considering. It comes from a rather unexpected source, from a statement of the saint not usually associated with a very open or progressive image of him. I refer to his "Rules for Thinking with the Church," an appendix of the *Spiritual Exercises*.[47] According to the best authorities, these eighteen concise rules were drafted during Ignatius' Paris years, and Father Dudon makes a very convincing case that they were inspired by the decrees of the Council of Sens, held at Paris in 1528, and by the writings of Josse Clichtove who was active at the council and more generally in the defense of Catholic doctrine against the Lutheran teachings.[48] Nearly all admit that they are specifically anti-Protestant, and indeed their whole thrust is to inculcate obedience to the Church and respect for traditional Catholic observances. Several of the rules—such as number six, praising the veneration of the relics of the saints, or number seven, praising the precepts concerning fast and abstinence —would seem to dissociate Ignatius from some of Erasmus' sharpest criticism, but too much, I believe, should not be made of this. Above all these "Rules" must not be read as a kind of anti-Erasmian or anti-humanist manifesto. The clearest proof of this is rule eleven in which Ignatius urges us "to praise both positive and scholastic theology." In that simple, unpretentious rule, the full import of which may be missed by those who fail to read it in the context of its times, the saint accepts with one decisive gesture the heart of Christian humanism—the renewal of theology through a return to Holy Scripture and the Fathers. He combines this, it is true, with the acceptance of a sound scholasticism, based above all on St. Thomas. By glaring omission he rejects the nominalism of Montaigu, Béda, and the Sorbonne. In short, he finds his footing amid the swirling intellectual currents of his day, and he lays the base for a creative and constructive synthesis. It will not be amiss to recall that after he finished his arts course at Sainte-Barbe Ignatius studied theology at the Dominican convent on the rue Saint-Jacques.[49] It was in this famous school that under Pierre Crockaert a revival of St. Thomas had begun in the early years of the century. Ignatius' position then as reflected in rule eleven associates him more with the theological approach of Cajetan or Contarini than with the anti-humanism of Béda, and indeed it will come as no surprise to discover that when the saint finally came to Rome at the end of 1537 he found in Cardinal Contarini the champion of his apostolate and his new Society.[50]

The "Rules" offer still another indication of the moderate and balanced attitude of Ignatius during these Paris years. Protestantism had become a serious problem and a threat in France, though the crisis did not appear grave enough in the eyes of Ignatius and his companions to deter them from their plan—Ignatius' original desire—to go to the East to evangelize the Turks. They solemnly vowed to do precisely that in a chapel on Montmartre in August 1534. This intention and vocation are in themselves very interesting facts, given all that was happening in Christian Europe in these very days. But just as interesting is the tone of rules fourteen through seventeen. Ignatius counsels us to be careful of the way we discuss the controversial questions of faith and grace. In these injunctions he is truly the master of calm, cooling, and deliberate understatement. Would that both sides had listened to him! And in rule seventeen he states:

Also in our discourse we ought not to emphasize the doctrine that would destroy free will. We may therefore speak of faith and grace to the extent that God enables us to do so, for the greater praise of His Divine Majesty. But, in these dangerous times of ours, it must not be done in such a way that good works or free will suffer any detriment or be considered worthless.

This position, I submit, in tone and in substance is remarkably close to the position of Erasmus. I do not say it was borrowed from him, but I do hold the view that it indicates, as do so many other comparable instances, that Ignatius was not so far from the fundamental spirit of Erasmus as we are often led to believe.

Since I wrote the above essay in the fall of 1967 several studies relevant to this theme have come to my attention, and I should like to take note of them at least in this concluding postscript. They are Marcel Bataillon, "D'Erasme à la Compagnie de Jésus," *Archives de sociologie des religions,* 24 (1967), 57–81; H. O. Evennett, *The Spirit of the Counter-Reformation,* ed. John Bossy (Cambridge, 1968); Mark Rotsaert, "Les premiers contacts de saint Ignace avec l'érasmisme espagnol," *Revue d'histoire de la spiritualité,* 49 (1973), 4, 443–64; Terence O'Reilly, "Saint Ignatius Loyola and Spanish Erasmianism," *Archivum Historicum Societatis Iesu,* 43 (1974), 301–20; and A. H. T. Levi, "Erasmus, the Early Jesuits and the Classics," in *Classical Influences on European Culture, A.D. 1500–1700,* ed. R. R. Bolgar (Cambridge, 1976), pp. 223–38. The number and quality of these studies underscore, I think, the importance of our topic, and they reveal too the broad and complex character of the relationship between Erasmus and Ignatius, a relationship which continues to be somewhat controversial.

Bataillon's article, elaborating references to St. Ignatius and the young Society in his *Erasme et l'Espagne,* particularly the thesis that the Society of Jesus was a major departure from monastic tradition and reflected the Erasmian dictum *Monachatus non est pietas,* takes up many of the points I have discussed and is generally corroborative of the view I have developed. He gives, however, another and very interesting explanation for the drafting of the "Rules for Thinking with the Church." He sees them as an affirmation of orthodoxy occasioned by the need to protect the young Society in the face of the opposition it met from Cardinals Ghinucci and Guidiccioni when papal approval was being sought in 1539–40. Indeed this may in part be the case, but the significance of the "Rules" as well as their scope, I believe, extends far beyond this single though very critical occasion.

Evennett's work (the posthumous publication of his Birkbeck Lectures at the University of Cambridge in 1951) covers a much larger subject than my or Bataillon's theme, but it lays great stress on the role of Ignatius and his Society in the development of Catholic reform, and it discusses at length the character of Ignatian spirituality (chap. III) and the features of the new religious Order (chap. IV). Evennett places both in the context of their times, linking Ignatius' spiritual formation to the influence of the *Devotio moderna* and the Society to contemporary currents and needs. He treats the specific question of Erasmus' influence rather gingerly (pp. 54–55, 63–64, 74–77), but the whole approach and tenor of his study tend to substantiate the general view I have expressed.

Rotsaert's analysis is very similar to mine. He sees a *parallélisme* between the *Enchiridion* and the *Spiritual Exercises* on several points, and he comes to the conclusion that the difference between Erasmus and St. Ignatius lies not on the level of the elements which constitute their spirituality but on the level of the quality or intensity of that spirituality, Ignatius having undergone a profound personal experience. At the outset he stresses a most important point—namely, that our understanding of the relationship between the two men depends on our view of each of them. Rotsaert's own view of Erasmus, for example, is in line with the work of more recent scholars, such as Massaut and Chantraine, who have emphasized the theological substance and depth of the humanist's religious thought. Erasmus' congruity with Ignatius, then, is not difficult to conceive of. By the same token those who have followed an older interpretation of Erasmus and have found his Catholicism dubious and suspect will draw a sharp contrast between the two men and point up their essential differences.

O'Reilly's article fits into this latter category. Reviewing the state of the question he focuses on a comparison of the *Spiritual Exercises* with the *Enchiridion*. His analysis is quite different from Rotsaert's. He sees a fundamental dissimilarity in the thought or spirituality of the two men, linking Erasmus with the classical Renaissance and Ignatius with a more fervent medieval religious tradition. In his view other reform currents in Spain and not Erasmianism (as Bataillon maintains) influenced Ignatius.

Levi takes the opposite tack. His essay discusses two chief points of congruence between Erasmus and St. Ignatius, one of which is original and not observed or taken into account by the many other analysts of this relationship. He sees a great similarity between a passage in a preface to Erasmus' *Paraphrasis in Evangelium Matthaei* and Ignatius' doctrine of the discernment of spirits, and he holds that "it is impossible to deny some form of influence" between this text and the *Spiritual Exercises.* Levi's other major point is that Ignatius and the early Jesuits shared Erasmus' view of the ancient classics and their importance in Christian education and man's moral reformation. "Their styles were totally different [Levi writes]. But their guiding principles and their views of human nature, as illustrated in their attitudes to the major classical authors, were not so very different, as both were nourished in the same evangelical and partly illuminist tradition, and the one influenced the other more than has ever been admitted."

NOTES

1. The question, of course, is not entirely original. Henri Brémond in the opening pages of his *Histoire littéraire du sentiment religieux en France depuis la fin des guerres de religion jusqu'à nos jours* (11 vols.; Paris, 1916–33), I, saw a close relationship between the early Jesuits and the tradition of Christian humanism, and Marcel Bataillon in *Erasme et l'Espagne* (Paris, 1937), pp. 229–31, strongly suggests the influence of Erasmus on Ignatius. I mention these two authors in particular as directing my own thought to the problem. There is also some literature on the subject, notably R. G. Villoslada, s.j., "San Ignacio de Loyola y Erasmo de Rotterdam," *Estudios eclesiasticos*, 16 (1942), 235–64, 399–426, and 17 (1943), 75–103, a lengthy analysis taking issue with Bataillon, and M. Olphe-Galliard, s.j., "Erasme et Ignace de Loyola," *Revue d'ascétique et de mystique*, 35 (1959), 337–52, an excellent bibliographical article. Father Villoslada's study, amplified and revised, has been published in book form, *Loyola y Erasmo, dos almas, dos epocas* (Madrid, 1965), though I have not used or cited this work.

2. On the life of St. Ignatius, see James Brodrick, s.j., *The Origin of the Jesuits* (New York, 1940) and *Saint Ignatius Loyola, the Pilgrim Years, 1491–1538* (New York, 1956), and Paul Dudon, s.j., *St. Ignatius of Loyola*, trans. William J. Young, s.j. (Milwaukee, 1949). See also *The Autobiography of St. Ignatius Loyola*, trans. Joseph F. O'Callaghan, ed. John C. Olin (New York, 1974). The earliest *vitae* and the basic sources for his life are in *Fontes narrativi de S. Ignatio de Loyola* (4 vols.; Rome, 1943–65), a section of the voluminous *Monumenta Historica Societatis Iesu.* There are two very useful bibliographies for Ignatius: Jean-François Gilmont, s.j., and Paul Daman, s.j., *Bibliographie ignatienne (1894–1957)* (Paris–Louvain, 1958), and I. Iparraguirre, s.j., *Orientaciones bibliográficas sobre San Ignacio de Loyola* (2nd ed.; Rome, 1965).

3. On the Manresa experience, see especially *The Autobiography of St. Ignatius Loyola*, Chap. 3, and Hugo Rahner, s.j., *The Spirituality of St. Ignatius Loyola*, trans. William J. Young, s.j. (Westminster, Md., 1953).

4. *The Autobiography of St. Ignatius Loyola*, p. 54.

5. In his *Vita Ignatii Loiolae*, Book I, Chap. XIII, a work written in 1567–69 and first published in Naples in 1572. There were many subsequent editions, and Ribadeneira himself translated it into Spanish and first published this version in Madrid

in 1583. The critical edition of the Latin and Spanish texts is in *Fontes narrativi de S. Ignatio de Loyola*, IV; pp. 172–75 give the account of the reading.

Ribadeneira (1526–1611) met Ignatius in Rome in 1540, and he entered the Society of Jesus that same year, its founding year, an extremely young novice indeed. His studies occupied the next several years and took him to Paris in 1542 and to Padua in 1545–49. He taught in Palermo 1549–52 and was made principal of the new Germanicum in Rome in 1552. He was one of Ignatius' closest associates in the last years of the saint's life. See *Enciclopedia Universal Ilustrada Europeo-Americana*, LI, 292–93, and also Jean-François Gilmont, s.j., *Les écrits spirituels des premiers Jésuits* (Rome, 1961), pp. 32–33, 269–76.

6. This is quite clear, I believe, from Father Villoslada's articles in *Estudios eclesiásticos* and from Father Brodrick's *Saint Ignatius Loyola, the Pilgrim Years*, where (pp. 156–63) Ribadeneira's account is followed and much is made of the contrast between the two men. Father Brodrick's sketch of Erasmus in these pages, I might add, is a caricature.

7. *Fontes narrativi de S. Ignatio de Loyola*, I, 669. There is another entry substantially the same in González' Memorial, ibid., I, 585, but this was made as an annotation in Portuguese many years later. The original enry of 1555, it will be noted, is a much earlier text than Ribadeneira's and actually dates from Ignatius' own lifetime (he died July 31, 1556). See Gilmont, op. cit., pp. 37–38.

8. Bataillon, op. cit., pp. 229–30, and Dudon, op. cit., p. 107. Dudon makes reference to Polanco rather than to Ribadeneira, i.e. to Juan Polanco, *Vita Ignatii Loiolae et rerum Societatis Jesu historia*, where substantially the same story is told about Ignatius' reading the *Enchiridion* in Barcelona. See *Fontes narrativi*, II, 543. Polanco, however, wrote his *Vita* in 1574 and took the story about Ignatius and the *Enchiridion* from Ribadeneira.

9. *The Autobiography of St. Ignatius Loyola*, p. 73.

10. On the Castilian version of the *Enchiridion*, see Bataillon, op. cit., pp. 205ff.

11. *The Autobiography of St. Ignatius Loyola*, p. 61. See also Villoslada, op. cit., 16: 255–56, 260–61.

12. Bataillon, op. cit., p. 230. González de Cámara specifically mentions Miona as the confessor who recommended the reading of the *Enchiridion*, in *Fontes narrativi*, I, 585. Miona entered the Society of Jesus in 1545.

13. Father Villoslada, op. cit., 16:238, 241ff. frankly acknowledges this—an admission, in my judgment, which seriously undercuts his thesis.

14. Joseph de Guibert, s.j., *The Jesuits, Their Spiritual Doctrine and Practice*, trans. William J. Young, s.j. (Chicago, 1964), pp. 155–56.

15. *The Autobiography of St. Ignatius Loyola*, pp. 39–40.

16. Father Villoslada also acknowledges this, although he himself does not hold that Ignatius borrowed it. See his work, 16:244–48. The statement of H. R. Trevor-Roper in his essay on Erasmus that "Loyola himself had read Erasmus' *Enchiridion*, and he based his *Spiritual Exercises* fundamentally upon it," in *Historical Essays* (New York, 1966), p. 57, is, of course, a gross exaggeration.

17. Erasmus, *The Enchiridion*, trans. Raymond Himelick (Bloomington, 1963), pp. 94–101.

18. St. Ignatius, *The Spiritual Exercises*, trans. Anthony Mottola (New York, 1964), pp. 47–48. The rule is stated elsewhere at key places in the *Exercises*, e.g. the

third class of men, p. 78, the second mode of humility, p. 82, the election, pp. 82–83.

It is not possible to date the *Spiritual Exercises* or the composition of its various parts with precision. The book as we have it today developed in the period between Manresa (1522) and the time Ignatius left Paris (1535). The "first week" was substantially complete when the saint was at Alcalá, though we do not know if the Principle and Foundation had then been drafted. That latter rule probably dates from his Paris years, though that in itself does not rule out the actual origin of it at Alcalá. On the earliest texts of the *Spiritual Exercises*, see Gilmont, op. cit., Chap. II.

19. For another example on the part of Erasmus of an Ignatian-like spirit of indifference toward created things I should like to call attention to his colloquy "The Well-to-do Beggars," first published in 1524. There are also a few points in that colloquy which suggest the young Society of Jesus. See Erasmus, *The Colloquies*, trans. Craig R. Thompson (Chicago, 1965), pp. 203–17.

20. Bataillon, op. cit., p. 230.

21. *Ibid.*, p. 747. It was one of the main points raised by Cardinal Ghinucci in his objections to the plan of the new Society when papal approval was being discussed in 1540, and it continued to be a major point at issue among those who were hostile to the early Jesuits. After Gian Pietro Carafa (with whom Ignatius had long had serious differences) became Pope Paul IV in 1555, he imposed the obligation of choir, though it was subsequently revoked.

22. In this regard I should like to call attention to Ignatius' famous Letter to the Fathers and Brothers of Coimbra, May 7, 1547, reprinted in *Readings in Church History*, ed. Colman J. Barry, o.s.b. (Westminster, Md., 1965), II, 112–19.

23. This feature can be said to be especially significant in view of Erasmus' persistent criticism that young men were hustled into the monastic life before they had the chance to make a free and fair decision. One might also note the emphasis Ignatius gives in the *Spiritual Exercises* to the election, i.e. to the "wise and good" choice of a way of life. It is the very focal point of his discipline.

24. Another very significant feature in view of a criticism Erasmus constantly makes. See for instance "The Well-to-do Beggars."

25. *Monumenta Historica Societatis Iesu*, Litterae quadrimestres, I (Madrid, 1897), 349–58.

26. Allan P. Farrell, s.j., *The Jesuit Code of Liberal Education* (Milwaukee, 1938), Chaps. I and II. On the character of Jesuit education, so thoroughly humanist, see François de Dainville, s.j., *La naissance du l'humanisme moderne* (Paris, 1940), Vol. I: *Les Jésuits et l'humanisme* (the only volume published of this interesting work).

27. Du Coudray also says that Nadal (who was the rector at Messina) thought it possible to use Lorenzo Valla in the advanced grammar class and that in dialectics where Aristotle was studied the works either of George of Trebizond or Jacques Lefèvre were used. The college had a remarkably humanist orientation indeed.

28. The pertinent texts are quoted and discussed in Villoslada, op. cit., 17:88–100. Villoslada readily admits that Erasmus was widely used in the Jesuit colleges and that "Saint Ignatius never dictated to the Company a law or general decree against Erasmian books" (p. 96).

29. *Ibid.*, 92. Brodrick, *Saint Ignatius Loyola, the Pilgrim Years*, p. 228, also quotes this letter, and he concludes that "Ignatius never forbade the reading of Erasmus and Vives outright, but merely discountenanced it."

30. Villoslada, op. cit., 17:96–97, and Bataillon, op. cit., p. 587.

31. A situation signaled and described in *ibid.*, Chap. XIII: *L'érasmisme condamné*. A kind of climax was reached in the *Index* of Paul IV in 1558 which held Erasmus to be a heretic *primae classis* and condemned all his works (*ibid.*, p. 760). The Spanish *Index* of 1559 was a bit less draconian, but it prohibited a good portion of his writing, including the *Enchiridion* (*ibid.*, pp. 762–63).

32. The only reference to Erasmus in Ribadeneira's *Vita Ignatii Loiolae* other than the one we have been discussing is a brief remark toward the end of his work (Book V, Chap. X) that Ignatius did not want the Society to read authors like Erasmus, *dubii ac suspecti*, and Ribadeneira adds that Ignatius was of this opinion "long before they were censured by the Apostolic See." The chapter where this information is given us is entitled "Prudence in Spiritual Matters." *Fontes narrativi*, IV, 858–61.

33. Polanco, who in his *Vita Ignatii Loiolae* repeats substantially the same story Ribadeneira tells about Ignatius and the *Enchiridion* (see n. 8), adds, however, that Ignatius prohibited the reading of Erasmus in the Society "when he afterward became still better acquainted with the spirit of Erasmus" (*Fontes narrativi*, II, 543). Both authors are in error about the prohibition, but at least Polanco does not connect it with the early reading of the *Enchiridion*.

34. This criticism of Ribadeneira is, of course, quite aside from the fact that the author was not born until 1526, the year Ignatius came to Alcalá. His story at best could be based only on a later recollection.

It need hardly be pointed out that our criticism of Ribadeneira in this instance also applies to Polanco and, for that matter, to Gian Pietro Maffei, whose life of Ignatius, first published in 1585, follows Polanco.

35. Besides the biographies of Ignatius by Brodrick and Dudon, the following articles are excellent on Ignatius' Paris years: H. Bernard-Maître, s.j., "Les fondateurs de la Compagnie de Jésus et l'humanisme parisien de la Renaissance," *Nouvelle Revue Théologique*, 72 (1950), 811–23; I. Rodriguez-Grahit, "Ignace de Loyola et le collège Montaigu. L'influence de Standonck sur Ignace," *Bibliothèque d'Humanisme et Renaissance*, XX (1958), 388–401; and Robert Rouquette, s.j., "Ignace de Loyola dans le Paris intellectual du XVIe siècle," *Études*, 290 (1956), 18–40.

36. On the two Gouveas, see Marcel Bataillon, *Études sur le Portugal au temps de l'humanisme* (Coimbra, 1952), pp. 109–29.

37. Bernard-Maître, op. cit., pp. 821–23, 830.

38. Rouquette, op. cit., p. 30.

39. *Fontes narrativi*, II, 557–58. The text is quoted and discussed also in Villoslada, op. cit., 17:82–85, and Broderick, *Saint Ignatius Loyola, the Pilgrim Years*, pp. 226–27. Polanco's *Vita Ignatii Loiolae*, which was written in 1574, is our only source for this story.

40. Brodrick, *Saint Ignatius Loyola, the Pilgrim Years*, p. 227.

41. Dudon, op. cit., pp. 133–34.

42. Notably in his *In pseudo-dialecticos* of 1520. See Bataillon, *Erasme et l'Espagne*, pp. 18–19, 108–9, et passim.

43. I presume that Vives knew the Gouveas as well as the humanist scholar Juan Gelida, a Valencian like himself. It may be interesting to investigate these relationships.

As a postscript to the story of Ignatius' visit to the home of Vives, I might note that Ignatius also paid a visit to the home of the Portuguese humanist Damião de Gois in Padua ca. 1537. It appears to have been occasioned by an argument that Ignatius' companion Simon Rodriguez had with Gois. Ignatius came to apologize. See Bataillon, *Études sur le Portugal*, p. 255 n. 1, and Elisabeth Feist Hirsch, *Damião de Gois, the Life and Thought of a Portuguese Humanist, 1502–1574* (The Hague, 1967), p. 96.

44. Helyar's text is in *Monumenta Ignatiana, Exercitia Spiritualia* (Madrid, 1919), pp. 624–48. On Helyar, see Herbert Thurston, s.j., "The First Englishman to Make the *Spiritual Exercises,*" *The Month*, 142 (1923), 336–47, and Henry de Vocht, "John Helyar, Vives' Disciple," *Humanistica Lovaniensia*, 4 (1934), 587–608.

45. Joseph Crehan, s.j., "Saint Ignatius and Cardinal Pole," *Archivum Historicum Societatis Iesu*, 25 (1956), 73–75.

46. Bataillon, *Erasme et l'Espagne*, pp. 631–32. See also de Guibert, op. cit., pp. 164–65. Father de Guibert notes "the undeniable similarity in many features between the ideas of Ignatius and those of these spiritual humanists," i.e. Erasmus, Vives, Lefèvre, and he feels that this similarity is due to a common source, namely, the *Devotio moderna*. Indeed I believe this is a very large part of the story. With regard to the influence of the *Devotio* on Ignatius I should like to call attention to I. Rodriguez-Grahit, "La *Devotio moderna* en Espagne et l'influence française," *Bibliothèque d'Humanisme et Renaissance*, 19 (1957), 489–95.

47. St. Ignatius, *The Spiritual Exercises* (ed. cit.), pp. 139–42.

48. Dudon, op. cit., pp. 146, 457–62.

49. *Ibid.*, pp. 143–45, and Rouquette, op. cit., pp. 31–32.

50. See the extremely interesting article by Angel Suquia, "Las reglas para sentir con la iglesia en la vida y en las obras del Cardenal Gaspar Contarini (1483–1542)," *Archivum Historicum Societatis Iesu*, 25 (1956), 380–95.

ERASMUS' LETTER TO CARONDELET
The Preface to His Edition of St. Hilary of Poitiers, 1523

THIS PREFACE is in the form of a dedicatory letter to Jean de Carondelet, a high
official at the Hapsburg court in the Low Countries. It first appeared in the
large folio edition of the works of St. Hilary of Poitiers which Erasmus edited
and Johann Froben published in Basel in February 1523. Carondelet belonged
to a prominent Burgundian family whose members had long served the Haps-
burgs in many posts. He had been a secretary to the young Charles V, and at
the time of Erasmus' dedication he was chief counselor to Margaret of Austria,
Charles' aunt and his regent in the Low Countries. He had also been appointed
Archbishop of Palermo in 1519, although the appointment was contested and
he never resided in that primatial see.

The patristic edition which the essay introduces contains the work of the
fourth-century Father and Bishop of Poitiers who had led the fight against the
Arian heresy in the West. His years are ca. 315 to 367, and he was one of the
earliest and most important western Fathers. Most of his works were composed
in the context of the Arian struggle, and Erasmus in his preface uses the
example of St. Hilary or at least the occasion of his role in that widespread
controversy to draw certain lessons about doctrinal controversy in general and
the recently arisen Lutheran controversy in particular. It is this aspect of the
essay which gave it a special thrust in its own day and which continues to render
it of considerable interest and importance. Indeed it contains some of Erasmus'
most pungent comments on the nature of theology and on the baleful consequences of theological argument and contention. "The sum and substance of
our religion is peace and concord," he tells us in a frequently quoted sentence
from the preface, and his recurrent theme is that excessive theologizing destroys
the unanimity that should exist among Christians whose faith ought to be
manifested in their lives rather than in their debates and quarrels. "Once faith
was more a matter of a way of life than of a profession of articles," he declares
in another memorable passage. The significance of this familiar Erasmian
message restated so forcefully in the midst of the religious crisis which had
now developed can easily be grasped. And it seems quite evident too that Erasmus has taken this opportunity to expound and defend his point of view before Carondelet and other influential friends.

The preface, however, gave Erasmus' critics additional cause for anger and
complaint. The Sorbonne censured several passages from it in 1526. These
were passages generally in which Erasmus impugned scholastic theology and

excessive dogmatic definition, and the *censurae* corrected his "errors" and accused him of following the heretics.* The following year at a conference of theologians at Valladolid in Spain which had been called specifically to examine certain writings of Erasmus several other passages were vehemently attacked.†
These dealt chiefly with statements about the Holy Spirit or contained Erasmus' comments on St. Hilary's references to the Holy Spirit in his *De Trinitate*.
He was accused of questioning the divinity of the Holy Spirit and of denying the Trinity. The Valladolid conference did not condemn Erasmus, but some very serious charges were hurled against him. The essay thus became one of Erasmus' more controversial writings, and the great Maurist edition of Hilary's works in 1693 still warned of Erasmus' preface and of his misrepresentation of the words and role of St. Hilary.‡

Erasmus' edition of St. Hilary was one of the dozen or more patristic editions which the great scholar prepared, beginning with the edition of St. Jerome published by Froben in 1516. These form the largest and certainly one of the most important segments of his life's work. His achievement in this field was to produce more accurate and more complete editions than had heretofore been available. In most cases the prefaces to these editions were notable essays containing incisive comments on the Father and his work as well as observations relevant to Erasmus' own aims and his own times. He was a scholar deeply involved in the issues and problems of his day, and his editorial activity had a very definite reform purpose. He was seeking nothing less than a renewal of theology by a return to its scriptural and patristic sources.

His Hilary edition replaces an earlier volume of the *Opera* of the Father edited by Robert Fortuné and published by Josse Badius Ascensius in Paris in 1511. It appears that Erasmus based his edition on this earlier one collating it with certain manuscripts and either correcting it or more frequently noting in the margin the variant readings and additions to the text which he had found.
The only manuscript we have any specific reference to is one which had been sent to Froben by Maternus Hatten, vicar of the cathedral of Speyer, in May 1522.§ A revised edition was brought out by the Froben firm in 1535, and subsequent revisions were published in Paris in 1544 and in Basel in 1550. Erasmus considered his dedicatory letter to Carondelet an important one and asked to have it included among the *epistolae* in his own *Opera omnia*.¶

---

* *Collectio judiciorum de novis erroribus*, ed. Charles du Plessis d'Argentré (3 vols.; Paris, 1728–36), II, 73, 76–77. The censured passages are indicated in the text.

† Marcel Bataillon, *Erasme et l'Espagne* (Paris, 1937), Chap. V, and Allen, VI, 471. The passages criticized at Valladolid are also indicated in the text.

‡ See Migne, *PL*, IX, 14–15.

§ Allen, V, 73.

¶ The following English translation of this letter was made by James F. Brady and John C. Olin from the Latin text in Allen, V, 173–92. It is the first time an English version has been published. For an analysis of this letter, see John C. Olin, "Erasmus and His Edition of St. Hilary," *Erasmus in English*, 9 (1978), 8–11.

To the most reverend Father in Christ and Lord, JEAN CARONDELET, *Archbishop of Palermo, Highest Counselor of the Imperial Court in Brabant, greetings from* ERASMUS OF ROTTERDAM

UNLESS the word Destiny is entirely meaningless, most illustrious Prelate, indeed I think I am destined to return again and again into labyrinths of the kind from which comes a great deal of vexation and weariness but the least possible measure of glory. In fact, without actual experience no one will believe, unless he personally has made the test, what effort he must expend who tries to emend the text of ancient authors which have been corrupted in various ways through fault of the times and copyists but above all because of the rashness of half-learned and foolhardy men. But it seems to me to be a mark of a great and lofty spirit publicly to serve all well even without the expectation of receiving thanks for such service. Further, it is the mark of even a loftier spirit and one which is wholly regal, as the saying goes, to be ill spoken of when one has done something worthwhile. And I would be more vexed that this has happened so often to me if I did not observe that the same thing has happened not only to all who have tried by their own industry to do something notably useful in the affairs of men, but even to St. Jerome himself whose learning or holiness is unsurpassed in the Latin world.

I had found the editing of Jerome's works a very arduous task, but editing Hilary's text entailed even greater labor. The latter's style, even where the subject matter itself is clear, is difficult to understand and susceptible to corruption. What, then, do you think was the nature of the task, when in that peculiar style of his he discusses rather than explains matters which are not only very difficult but even inexplicable? Yet scarcely in the case of another author has the rashness of the half-learned allowed itself greater liberty, and that especially with regard to *De Trinitate* and *De Synodis*. Because theological problems fraught with danger are treated in these works the greatest care must be taken, nor must the slightest change be made. If we discover after comparing different copies that in some places prefatory remarks have been added to the beginning of chapters and also flourishes at the end and that in the middle patches have been sewn on, we are discovering that in some places some one with little learning has tried to explain more completely and clearly what Hilary in his own fashion had said. On some pages twenty or thirty lines had been added.[1]

How often they excise passages which seemed at variance with the opinions accepted among the orthodox. Indeed in more than twenty places they had compounded a remedy, especially where he debates about the pains and torments which affected the body and soul of our Lord Jesus Christ. He does this in several places but chiefly in the tenth book of *De Trinitate*, though so confusedly that sometimes he clearly seems to attribute to Christ a body and soul subject to no troublesome conditions. When, to illustrate this, he used the comparison of a weapon penetrating water or fire by a violent thrust without the sign of a wound because the body attacked is not susceptible of a wound, although it is the nature of a weapon to inflict a wound, someone took it upon himself to add the qualification "if however this comparison can aptly be made." Again when a little later he added that "that body of the Lord may indeed have had pain similar in nature to ours, if our body is so constituted that it treads upon the waves and walks upon the waters," etc., concluding from this difference undoubtedly that the body of Jesus even in the sensation of pain was unlike our bodies, they had corrected the text to read as follows: "That body of the Lord may indeed have had (because of sin) pain similar in nature to ours, if our body is so constituted that it treads upon the waves (by its own nature or by the extraordinary help of God) and walks upon the waters," etc.[2]

A little later when St. Hilary had written, "And that man is from God, having indeed a body to suffer, and He did suffer, but not having a nature to feel pain," the passage was corrected, that is, corrupted, in this way: "And He did suffer, but not having a nature (weak because of sin like ours) to feel pain." Further on where Hilary had written, "The opinion based on human judgment therefore that He feels pain because He suffers is mistaken," they emended the wording thus: "That He (as if in the flesh of sin) feels pain because He suffers."[3] Likewise at the end of the second book when it was written as follows: "Therefore we must seek this Holy Spirit, we must deserve Him, and then we must hold Him by that faithfulness to and observance of the commandments," they had woven in, "we must deserve Him, we must adore Him." They feared undoubtedly that someone might suspect that he thought the Holy Spirit should not be adored when he teaches in many ways that the Father and the Son should be adored but makes no such pronouncement about the Spirit. Evidently this was because it did not come to his mind or because at that time this had not yet been precisely defined.

It is amazing, however, that the same individuals did not also corrupt the end of this work where consistently it is written: "May I adore you, our Father, and your Son together with you, and may I be deserving of your Holy Spirit who is from you through the only begotten Son." For here also when he declares that the Father and the Son "should be adored," he says only that the Holy Spirit "should be deserved." We have discovered such additions in more than thirty places in Hilary, although we have cited no more than one or two passages as examples to avoid irritating the reader. Again I am amazed that when he writes that the Holy Spirit is from the Father through the Son and that He does not proceed from both, it was not also corrected. Indeed in one particular text I discovered this correction: *through Him* was changed to *with Him*.

Now what is this rashness shown toward the writings of others, especially those of ancient authors whose memory, as it should be, is sacred to us, I mean the readiness to erase, expunge, add to, delete, change, forge —when there is no personal risk—any author at will? Is the object of this to prevent anyone from thinking that there are any errors in the works of the ancients? Indeed whoever should try that would wash a brick, as they say.[4] God has willed that the happy state of freedom from error be reserved for the sacred books alone. Everyone else, however learned and keen sighted he may be, on occasion stumbles and gropes blindly. Obviously therefore all remember that they are human and as humans they are read by us, with discrimination, with judgment, and at the same time with indulgence. But if anything occurs in these writings which has the appearance of error, when the author has a different opinion, the work must not be contaminated, but scruples should be allayed by adding explanatory notes. Peter Lombard attempts this in very many places, at the same time citing and explaining several passages concerning the pain and fear of Christ in the third book of the *Sentences*.[5]

That famous epigrammatic poet does not tolerate him who wishes to show his cleverness in another's book.[6] But who would tolerate those who arrogate so much to themselves that they sew on their own patches in place of the genuine text wherever they please? It is a mark of courtesy to interpret a work properly. To change arbitrarily the actual words in the works of the ancients, however, is an act of rashness, not to say irreverence. And yet we discover that this has been done even in the books of St. Ambrose and in more than one place. If the risk to the writer must be taken into account when a text is changed, it would be more fitting to do this in the books of modern authors whom time has not yet placed outside the uncertainty of judgment, nor death thus far delivered from envy. Now almost too scrupulously fair toward the ancient writers, we distort certain passages which have nothing wrong with them in the authors of our own age and we interpret everything improperly, just as if such an exegete would not be likely to find even in the Pauline epistles something which he would be able to misrepresent as erroneous, as suspect of heresy, as scandalous, as irreverent.

But let us drop this subject. It is better that I briefly express my opinion about each of Hilary's works individually. He wrote the twelve books of *De Trinitate* when an exile in Phrygia where he had been banished by the faction of a certain Saturninus, bishop of Arles, which had circumvented the Emperor. Indeed the Arian faction had sunk its roots so widely, had become so strong, that the world for a long time wavered in doubt as to which cause it would espouse, especially when the Emperor Constantius by the use of exile, plundering, threats, and alarms forced men to go over to the side of the Arians. Wherefore Hilary complained to Caesar that it was shameful that men in an unprecedented fashion were being forced rather than persuaded to accept the faith, granting that the faith of the Arians was sincere. And indeed he himself testifies in several places that for a long time he was silent. He observed this silence either because the soul even of that great man felt some doubt amid such widespread discord in the world or because when there was no hope that the better side could win he thought it preferable to look to a calm silence rather than to exacerbate, not remove, the world's general depravity by untimely boldness. He seems to have exerted all his energy, however, to manifest and put forth in this work whatever he could by his natural ability, by his eloquence, and by his knowledge of Holy Scripture. For we see that it was usually the ambition of distinguished writers as well as of outstanding painters and sculptors to leave in some one work a finished and complete example of their art by which posterity might be able to evaluate what they would have been able to do, if they had wished to exert their fullest powers. Virgil seems to have attempted this in the *Georgics*, Ovid in his *Medea*, Cicero in *De Oratore*, Augustine in *The City of God*, Jerome in the *Commentaries on the Prophets*, Thomas Aquinas on the subject of the Eucharist, Bernard on the Canticle.

We are stimulated more to this effort if there should come to hand a theme which is not only lofty and important but also new and accordingly not hackneyed. Indeed the grandeur of a work besides permitting a lofty treatment also lends dignity of itself, and the newness adds to the charm. Moreover, the ancient authors philosophized very rarely about theological questions, and they did not dare to make any pronouncement about such matters which was not clearly set forth in those writings whose authority is inviolable to us. But the irreverent rashness of the Cerinthians and the Ebionites first drove John the Evangelist to commit to writing certain mysteries concerning the divine nature of Christ.[7] Later the elaborate subtlety of the Arians drove the orthodox to a greater necessity—namely, to discuss with great controversy the question of the extension of the divine nature, of the creation of the Son, of the adoption into the name of God, and then the matter of ὁμοούσιον and ὁμοιούσιον, and finally to formulate definitions about these matters.[8] Repeatedly the most saintly Hilary deplores this necessity, knowing full well how fraught with danger and how inimical to devotion it is to speak out on matters which are beyond discussion, to examine matters beyond understanding, to make pronouncements on matters beyond the grasp of the intelligence.[9] But St. Augustine was carried still farther on this sea, evidently because the joy of inquiry like a favorable breeze lured the rich talent of the man from one realm of thought to another. More restraint is exercised by Peter Lombard, who when he cites another's views does not lightly add anything of his own, or if he adds anything, he offers it with diffidence. At length the matter advanced to the point of irreverent audacity.

But may the ancients gain the pardon besought by those whom necessity has driven to this pass. On what pretext will we ask pardon for ourselves, we who raise so many meddlesome, not to say irreverent, questions concerning matters very far removed from our nature, and who formulate so many definitions about matters which could have been either ignored without loss of salvation or left in doubt?[10] Or is he not destined to have fellowship with the Father, Son, and Holy Spirit who cannot disentangle according to the method of philosophy what distinguishes the Father from the Son or the Holy Spirit from both or what the difference is between the generation of the Son from the Father and the procession of the Spirit? If I believe, as has been handed down, that the three are of one nature, what is the need of labored disputation? If I do not believe, no human reasons will convince me. And such a dangerous inquisitiveness has generally arisen in us from the study of philosophy, a fact which the illustrious Tertullian, the most learned by far of all the Latin theologians, has asserted in several places, although he himself was a philosopher of the first rank.

Socrates of Athens, to whom is attributed this famous axiom, "What is above us is of no concern to us," brought down philosophy from the contemplation of natural phenomena into the midst of human life and frequently quoted that line from Homer:

What evil and what good have been wrought in thy halls.[11]

Nevertheless, many things are apprehended with certainty concerning the nature of the stars, the motion of the celestial spheres, lightning, the winds, the rainbow, and similar phenomena, because either the bodily senses themselves or the observation of effects provide the beginnings of knowledge for matters of this nature, and the knowledge is especially pleasing and moves one at the same time to wonder and to love of the Maker. But yet because the wise man perceived that men sat idle all their lifetime in such study and neglected meanwhile what has greater relevance for us, he called down all study from the contemplation of natural phenomena to the consideration of morals.[12] But those questions which we investigate and which we define sometimes have not been recorded in Holy Scripture, so that even if they cannot be understood they must at least be believed; nor can they, as they stand, be proved by any satisfactory arguments or grasped by the intellect or even vaguely conceived of by like means. And after the richest talents have applied all their energy for a long time to the investigation of them, this at last is the final result of their effort: they realize they know nothing; and what is more they contribute nothing to the devout life. Thus nowhere more does that well-known passage of Paul apply, "Knowledge puffs up, charity builds up."[13]

What arrogance, what contentions, what tumult, what discord in the world do we see gush forth from this kind of absurd learning! Although our life is so fleeting, we neglect meanwhile those things without which no one has any hope of attaining salvation. Unless I pardon my brother's sins against me, God will not pardon my transgressions against Him. Unless I have a pure heart, I shall not see God. Therefore with all my energy I must aim, I must practice, I must strive to cleanse my soul of malice, envy, hatred, pride, avarice, and lust. You will not be damned if you should not know whether the Spirit proceeding from the Father and the Son has a single or a double principle, but you will not escape perdition unless you see to it in the meantime that you have the fruits of the Spirit, which are charity, joy, peace, patience, kindness, goodness, forbearance, gentleness, faith, moderation, self-control, and chastity.[14] Toward this end the chief concern of our study therefore must be focused and directed. Not that I think either that inquiry in the three divisions of philosophy or that the investigation of phenomena beyond this world should be entirely condemned, provided that the inquirer is endowed with rich talent and is purged of rashness in defining, of obstinacy, and of the bane of harmony, the stubborn passion to get the upper hand.

The sum and substance of our religion is peace and concord. This can hardly remain the case unless we define as few matters as possible and leave each individual's judgment free on many questions. This is because the obscurity of most questions is great and the malady is for the most part intrinsic to our human nature: we do not know how to yield once a question has been made a subject of contention. And after the debate has warmed up each one thinks that the side he has undertaken rashly to defend is absolute truth. In this regard certain men were so lacking in moderation that after defining everything in theology they—and they are no more than men—invented a new system of theology,[15] and this has aroused more questions and greater commotion in the world than the Arians in their foolishness once did. But certain pundits on some occasions are ashamed to have no rejoinder to make. On the contrary this is indeed the mark of theological learning: to define nothing beyond what is recorded in Holy Scripture, but to dispense in good faith what is there recorded.[16] Many puzzling questions are now referred to an Ecumenical Council. It would be much more fitting to defer such questions to that time when we shall see God face to face without the mirror and without the mystery.[17]

But these matters will be discussed perhaps more appropriately elsewhere. I now return to our main theme. The subject of Hilary's *De Trinitate* was especially magnificent and worthy of his lofty style, and it was new because, unless I am mistaken, Hilary was the first of the Latins to draw the sword of his eloquence against the Arians. That engagement also brought a great deal of fame to him chiefly because the issue was joined with a renowned foe. I do not doubt that several among the Greeks besides Athanasius did the same. But it was a practice of that age to cite no one by name with the exception of Holy Scripture, especially if the material was drawn from Greek sources, for these they claimed for themselves as if they had a right to them. In any case it seems to me to be the part of candor not to conceal the names of those whom you have used to your advantage. Hilary governs his expression throughout this work, however, as if he personally had dug each of his ideas out of the sacred books. And although I might have wished that such a talent, such an eloquence, such a mind might have richer and more fruitful material, nevertheless the profit to the reader from this work will also be not insignificant because he explains with no less felicity than accuracy, in my opinion, very many passages in John and Paul which are quite obscure.

Furthermore Jerome in a certain letter to Paulinus as he passes judgment on the learned writes that Hilary is distinguished by a lofty Gallic style although in other respects his manner is marked by the embellishments of the Greeks; he further says that he is read in vain by the more ignorant because he sometimes uses long involved periods.[18] Although everywhere Hilary has his own characteristic style, it is especially present in this work. For to the subject matter which, as is probable, he borrowed from the Greeks he has added Gallic grandiloquence; for a learned simplicity is characteristic of the Greeks, and a graceful and clear style is more to their liking than a lofty and labored one. And he often plays with standard themes [*loci communes*] such as the following: it is very risky to discuss theological questions; it is deplorable for a man to incur the shame of defending stubbornly in debate even an acknowledged error; Holy Scripture should not be twisted to our inclinations, but our way of thinking should be corrected in accordance with the norm of Scripture.[19] Moreover he frequently rises to what I might call the grandeur of theatrical embellishment, especially in those parts which easily lend themselves to brilliant expression, as for instance parts dealing with the structure of the universe, the nature of the heavenly bodies, the harmonious discord of the elements, the gush of springs, the course of rivers, the ebb and flow of the tides, and the various fruits of the earth. And not infrequently he rises to the grandeur of tragic figures, personification and apostrophe, by means of which he addresses either heretics or God Himself.

Perhaps this grandiloquence is a characteristic of the Gallic genius. Sulpicius Severus possesses something of this sort, and Eucherius also has it; the latter's is a grandiloquence which is even more elaborate but marked by a more felicitous care, if I am any judge.[20] Nor does Guillaume Budé, most renowned of the writers of this age, fail to reach the level of this style. His style is so elevated that one imagines one hears a trumpet sounding, not a man, and so felicitously finished that he never cloys the learned reader and keeps at a distance those who have only a rudimentary education. Furthermore obscurity of expression results, albeit only in part, from the fact that Hilary often barely rounds off in a long circuitous way a sentence composed of various clauses. Clarity, however, is also hindered by the fact that in handling a subject in itself involved and subtle he has also sought applause for his acumen and sometimes for his richness of style—a mannerism which likewise marks the writing of Budé in his *De asse*. But this disadvantage becomes easier to handle once you have become accustomed to it. For as you may have difficulty understanding certain speakers unless you hear them with some frequency, and as a type of music is less enjoyable for the very reason that it is new and unusual, so because each author has his own style that style becomes more familiar and therefore more pleasing by our becoming accustomed to it. Indeed even Titus Livy, the most pleasing of writers, is at first taste somewhat bitter. This happens, however, chiefly in the case of those authors who, aside from what I might call their individual flavor, bring to their work a capacity for taking pains and a striving for subtlety. Among orators of this kind Quintilian especially ought to be classed, and among poets Horace.

It appears that St. Jerome perceived this. He writes as follows in a letter to a Roman orator: "Hilary, a confessor of my times and a bishop, imitated the twelve books of Quintilian both in style and in number."[21] It is most difficult, however, for the man who either teaches the rules of an art or offers arguments on matters naturally subtle to combine a concern for polished style with clear expression. In addition to these difficulties Quintilian also strove for brevity. When I consider the varied diction of the ancient writers it seems that hardly any provincials successfully reproduce the simplicity of Roman speech except the few who were educated at Rome from boyhood. For both Tertullian and Apuleius have a style of their own, and in the decrees of the Africans, many of which Augustine refers to against Petilianus and Cresconius, you may observe an anxious striving for eloquence, but such is their style that you recognize their African origin. Augustine also sometimes is rather obscure and labored, nor is Cyprian entirely without African traits, although he is clearer than the others. Nor is it strange if a Gaul reflects something Gallic or a Carthaginian something Carthaginian when traces of Paduan idiom in Livy's Latin is offensive to some. Generally, however, the striving is greater in one whose command of a language is characteristic of provincials rather than citizens and who is a foreigner rather than native-born. Undoubtedly this is why that old woman, as the story goes, called Theophrastus a "foreigner" because his language was too Attic.[22]

Nevertheless, it seems to me indeed that St. Jerome is misusing the term "imitated" for one who is like or resembles another. For the child is like or resembles the parent rather than imitates him. But it is nature which in the production of offspring more truly imitates now the father, now the mother, now the grandfather or grandmother, now the aunt or uncle. Accordingly, imitation is a matter of effort, likeness is a result. Nor do we always resemble that which we imitate, and sometimes resemblance is unwitting. Moreover, though perhaps it may not be improper to emulate Quintilian's style, yet it would rightly seem characteristic of what I might call an over-anxious scrupulosity to have aimed at even the same number of books especially when the subject was different. For the rest, as Hilary is unlike Quintilian in the fullness of style (for he continually repeats and hammers home the same idea in different words), so he is almost in distress in imitating a concern for order, spending no little time in promising what he is going to say and in repeating what he has said (in this indeed he is more like Aristotle than Quintilian), and spending much time in devising transitions to make neat connections between the various parts and much time apologizing when, as the occasion arises, he touched on a topic which according to the division of contents he promised should have been treated in another place. In two respects he recalls Pliny who wrote a history of the world, first because of a preface which is too elaborate, secondly because he intended the first book, which, it appears, he wrote last, to be a catalogue of the entire work.

And so much for the work bearing the title *De Trinitate*. The *De Synodis* follows it and treats the same subject in another way. For it reports on those assemblies of bishops in which the heresy of the Arians was condemned. He wrote this work for the bishops of Gaul, congratulating them for holding back from the Arian faction amid such great confusion in the world. He translates it, as he himself testifies, from the Greek; he takes the liberty, however, of avoiding everywhere a word-for-word translation and only renders the thought, and where the opportunity presents itself he mixes in his own ingredients. He allows himself this liberty also in discussing the Psalms, as we shall soon explain in its proper place. Furthermore, although this book restates the synodal decisions, he nevertheless seeks to avoid the risk of defending them, not so much, I think, because he lacked confidence in those for whom he was writing *De Synodis* or because there were certain propositions of which he did not fully approve, but because of what I might call a scrupulous concern to avoid strong assertions, a concern which little by little we have so forgotten that nothing causes shame. For thus generally in the affairs of men a situation from modest beginnings gains greater significance until it proliferates into something evil. St. Hilary at the end of the twelfth book of *De Trinitate* does not dare to make any pronouncement about the Holy Spirit except that He is the Spirit of God—and it was unlikely that he would have dared to say this unless he had read it in Paul: he does not dare to use the word "creature" because he has not read it anywhere in Holy Scripture.[23]

This kind of profession would not be sufficient in this age because the needful diligence of the ancient Fathers has been very instructive for us, but we are carried far beyond what is needful. Once faith was more a matter of a way of life than of a profession of articles. Soon necessity inspired the imposition of articles, but these were few and apostolic in their moderation. Then the wickedness of the heretics made for a more precise examination of the sacred books, and intransigence necessitated the definition of certain matters by the authority of synods. Finally faith began to reside in the written word rather than in the soul, and there were almost as many faiths as men.[24] Articles increased, but sincerity decreased: contention boiled over, charity grew cold. The teachings of Christ, which in former times were not touched by the clash of words, began to depend on the support of philosophy: this was the first step of the Church on the downward path. There was an increase of wealth and an accretion of power. Furthermore, the intervention of imperial authority in this situation did not improve much the purity of faith. At length the consequence of all this was sophistical controversy and the eruption of thousands of articles. And then it became a matter of intimidation and threats. Although life may abandon us, although faith may be more on our lips than in our hearts, although that genuine understanding of Holy Scripture may fail us, yet we force men by intimidation to believe what they do not believe, to love what they do not love, and to understand what they do not understand. Compulsion is incompatible with sincerity, and nothing is pleasing to Christ unless it is voluntary.[25] St. Jerome calls to mind this work in a letter to Florentius, in these words: "I ask that you send me the very comprehensive book *De Synodis* of St. Hilary which I had copied with my own hand at Trier."[26]

Coupled with this is the book he wrote against the Emperor Constantius who favored the Arian faction, but he wrote this book against him, unless I am mistaken, after the Emperor had died. For he is reproached in strong terms, whereas two other books addressed to the same man —one written when he was alive; the other, it is believed, he also presented to him—are milder in tone. St. Jerome recalls this in the *Catalogus* [*scriptorum ecclesiasticorum*]: "Also there is that essay of his addressed to Constantius which he had presented to him when he was living in Constantinople. There is another one against Constantius which he wrote after his death." So much for Jerome. The harsher tone of the work against the deceased was due to religious devotion, the milder tone of his plea to the living was inspired by Christian prudence which prefers to cure an evil, should the opportunity be offered, rather than to aggravate it. But none of these books in my opinion should be considered finished. For although they promise a piece of work complete and developed in detail they do not fulfill their promise, but suddenly as it were they fall silent. Because of the similarity of subject matter there is joined to these an epistle written against Auxentius whom he prosecuted for his involvement in the Arian heresy at Milan.[27] The epistle of Auxentius in which he offers a defense of himself to the Emperors Valentinian and Valens accompanies it.

During my discussion of the foregoing the thought struck me in passing that perhaps some will be astonished that Hilary has scarcely anything to say about the Holy Spirit, although the thrust of so many books and so much zeal and effort and so many arguments, decisions, and anathemas is to make us believe that the Son is true God and of the same essence, or, as Hilary several times says, of the same genus and nature as the Father— the Greeks use the term ὁμοούσιον (that is, equal in power, wisdom, goodness, eternity, immortality, and all other attributes)—and although the entire controversy about the name of true God, about the term ὁμοούσιον, and about equality has no less a bearing on the Spirit than on the Son. Indeed nowhere does he write that the Holy Spirit must be adored and nowhere does he assign the word God to Him, save that in one or two passages in *De Synodis* he refers to those who dared to call the Father, Son, and Holy Spirit three Gods as condemned.[28] The reason was either that he thought at that time it was more important to defend the Son whose human nature made it more difficult to win assent to the divinity of Him who was also human—and the Arians were trying to rob Him of divinity, whereas the question about the Holy Spirit had not yet been raised—or that it was the scrupulous concern of the ancients that, although they worshiped God devoutly, they nevertheless did not dare to make any pronouncements about Him which were not explicitly set forth in the sacred books. Though in Scripture the name of God is several times assigned to the Son, yet nowhere is it explicitly assigned to the Holy Spirit.[29] It should be acknowledged, however, that the devout probing of the orthodox later ascertained with sufficient proof from Holy Scripture that whatever was attributed to the Son was appropriate to the Holy Spirit, except for the individuality of the Person. But because of the impenetrable obscurity of theological questions there existed reverential reluctance in assigning names: they thought it was wrong in theology to use words other than Holy Scripture used and the general authority of the Church handed down. They had read Holy Spirit, they had read the Spirit of God, they had read the Spirit of Christ. They had learned from the Gospel that the Holy Spirit is not separated from the Father and the Son. For the Apostles are taught to baptize in the name of the Father and of the Son and of the Holy Spirit. The fellowship of the three Persons is preserved in those short customary prayers left to us from the most ancient usage of the Church, at once brief and learned, in which the Father is addressed in prayer through the Son in the unity of the Holy Spirit. The Father is most frequently called God, the Son several times, the Holy Spirit explicitly never.

And these remarks of mine are not meant to call into question what has been handed down to us from Holy Scripture by the authority of the orthodox Fathers, but to show how much reverential reluctance the ancients had in making pronouncements in theology, although they had a greater devotion to theology than even we have—we who have rushed to such extremes of boldness that we have no scruples about dictating to the Son the way in which His mother should be honored. We dare to call the Holy Spirit true God, proceeding from the Father and the Son, which the ancients did not dare to do, but on the other hand we have no scruples about driving Him repeatedly out of the temple of our soul by our evil deeds, just as if it were our belief that the Holy Spirit is nothing more than a meaningless name.[30] By the same token the majority of the ancients who revered the Son with the greatest devotion nevertheless feared to use the term ὁμοούσιον because that term is nowhere used in Holy Scripture. Indeed the progress of the Church at first depended on purity of life rather than on an exact knowledge of the divine nature, and it has never sustained a greater loss than when it seemed to make the greatest possible advances in philosophical knowledge, yes, and in the things of this world, not because they are evil in themselves but because they frequently involve man in the cares of this world.

Nor is learning evil in itself, but it often begets factions and dissension. The defense of the Catholic faith is put forward as a pretext, and in the meantime personal feelings become involved and the devil's business is pursued in the name of Christ. I do not say this because I suspect anything of the sort about Hilary, which we certainly have found in the case of certain men of this age. Nevertheless, when he was alive he was a man; he did not lack human feelings; he could make mistakes, he could be misled. He had been banished and condemned by Saturninus; he spent several years in exile among the Phrygians, notorious for their uncivilized manners; he was hard-pressed in every way by the Arian faction. These influences and very many others could have played upon the feelings of even a good man under the guise of piety.

I do not deny that heretical intransigence must be abhorred, if incurable. But meanwhile because of our hatred of one error we must beware of falling into another. Let us preserve that self-control, to prevent controversy from convincing us that the straight is crooked and the bitter sweet and vice versa. If this has happened to nearly all the ancients to some extent, indeed I shall not be expressing disapproval of the character of a learned man in the remarks I am going to make. Tertullian while he fought too aggressively against those who set a higher value on marriage than was reasonable fell into another pitfall in condemning what Christ approved, and demanding what He did not demand but only recommended. Jerome fights with such excessive zeal against those who extolled marriage to the detriment of virginity that he himself with difficulty could defend his case in an unfriendly court, if he should be charged with treating wedlock and a second marriage without enough respect. Montanus in opposing rather vigorously those who opened the doors of the Church indiscriminately to the worthy and the unworthy at a time when there was an inordinate relaxation of Church discipline fell into the opposite error. St. Augustine in combating Pelagius with all his energy somewhere attributes less to free will than those who now reign in the theological schools think ought to be attributed.[31]

I could mention very many examples to illustrate this point even from modern authors, but it is better, I believe, not to be too wordy in dealing with an unpleasant subject. We now turn to the subject of Hilary who because of the sanctity of his life, because of his extraordinary learning, and because of his admirable eloquence was the light of his age. How great is the anger with which he attacks the Arians, again and again calling them impious, diabolic, blasphemous, devils, plagues, Antichrists! For already the label heretic is of little importance. And yet it is probable that there were men in the Arian faction who were convinced that their preaching about Christ was true and devout. Their doctrine rested on many and important authorities. Some passages in Holy Scripture gave the appearance of supporting it, and rational arguments were not lacking which displayed some semblance of truth. In addition there was the authority of Caesar and beyond that the huge number of adherents, which by right should have been added, if the majority were always the better side. Finally it was a controversy about matters far beyond human comprehension. I would have recommended that anyone in agreement with Arius be admonished and instructed, but I would not immediately have called him Satan or Antichrist.

Indeed if these accusations must be hurled against anyone who errs on some point, what shall we do with our Hilary himself, not to mention so many outstanding doctors of the Church—Hilary who in so many passages seems to think that Christ had a body which was not susceptible to pain, that hunger, thirst, weariness, and other states of this kind were not natural to it but were assumed? For he plainly wrote this in his exposition of Psalm 68, while in a council he pronounces an anathema against the man who would deny that the Father alone is called unborn God, as if the Holy Spirit either is not God or is also born Himself of the Father. No one may plead that in councils Hilary is simply repeating decisions already made and is not their author as well. For he makes the same statement in his own name in the twelfth book of *De Trinitate*, asserting that the

Father alone is unborn God, that the Son alone is begotten, not created, that the Holy Spirit proceeds from both in such a way that He can neither be said to be born nor yet be admitted to share the name of creature, which some assign to the Son, calling Him a creature, for we utterly condemn the term creature no less in the case of the Holy Spirit than in that of the Father and the Son. And both elsewhere and in the eighth book of *De Trinitate* he maintains with great vehemence that we also are one with the Father and the Son by nature and not by adoption or by consensus only. Again in the third book of his work, but more in the tenth book, he speaks in such a way about the body of Christ that apparently he thinks that the Virgin Mary contributed nothing of her own except the service of conception, pregnancy, and parturition, although the orthodox believe that Christ was conceived by the agency of the Spirit, it is true, but from the substance of the Virgin's body. And indeed there are other passages which demand a courteous and proper interpreter. But what law does he establish in his own case who becomes so furious with others?[32]

We say this by no means to dim the glory and damage the reputation of a very holy and learned man, but to warn the bishops and theologians of our day against allowing themselves to be caught unawares by the kind of thing we see happen to so great a man. First, it is the part of evangelical honesty to interpret fairly the deeds and writings of brothers. Then, if anyone has erred whom we cannot ignore, he should not at once be subjected to our wrath, since everyone errs, but an effort should be made to eliminate the error without hurting the person concerned. Finally, a neighbor should be admonished as we would wish to be admonished, if we had fallen into human error. Today we see some who falsely censure everything in the books of others, who vent what I might call their rage against the good name of a neighbor, although in their own books one finds clear blasphemies against Christ. This would be an idle comment, if I should not point out in reality that in the books of certain men, which in great numbers now for the past several years have rushed forth from every quarter as champions of the majesty of the Pope, there are notions openly insulting to Christ which at the same time give strong support to the dignity of a human being. If the actual facts should not provide conclusive confirmation for this, I would be an unreliable witness.

I do not condemn the zeal of those who with moderation defend the authority of the Pope against the seditious impudence of certain men; nevertheless I would prefer that the glory of Christ so flourish that it eclipse the glory of all the world, even of Peter and Paul, should it be possible, not only of the Roman Pontiff. For thus eclipsed we would truly be glorious, if we of ourselves were nothing, but Christ were all in all. However, I speak about a few who while they strive intemperately to claim for man his proper dignity have not been sufficiently mindful of the dignity of Christ to whom alone all dignity is owed. In matters like this, although a Maevius may excuse himself, toward others he is so fierce, so pitiless, and so unjust.[33] What judgment can there be in a matter in which hate is so unbridled? The sword of the Gospel's Word must always indeed be brandished against all wicked errors, and one should make every effort to combat heresies as they spring up. But this must be our first concern that what we rail at in others is not found in ourselves, and this must be our second that we not be corrupted by our own personal feelings and call what is good evil, what is sweet bitter, what is clear obscure. For this is the mark of stubbornness implanted in the temperaments of the majority of men that they never stop defending a statement they have once made on some occasion or other, even if they discover that they have been wrong. First, shame stands in the way. Through contention it leads to stubbornness, and at length stubbornness develops into a madness. As a consequence, while the dispute becomes violent on both sides, on both sides the truth is lost.[34] The error is called a schism if anyone diminishes the authority of the Roman Pontiff. But why is no one disturbed when some men, extraordinarily impudent and basely servile, attribute too much to that authority? If falsehood causes displeasure, why does it not cause displeasure everywhere? Finally, why is the assertion that the Virgin Mother is free from original sin heretical among the Dominicans, orthodox among the Scotists? Is this not tantamount to openly declaring that judgment has been corrupted? Is this "cutting a straight furrow" for the Word of God? We gladly use this Pauline word.[35] Therefore, let the eye of him who is ready to take the mote out of his brother's eye be clear and unclouded. Let us always keep before our eyes the gentleness of Him who, although He alone was free from all error, nevertheless did not extinguish the smoking flax, nor crush the bruised reed.[36] But these matters also will be discussed more appropriately elsewhere.

The *Commentaries on Matthew*, as Jerome calls them, come next. Others have preferred to call them a catalogue because, I believe, he expounds some headings separately. I do not doubt that he translated this work from Origen; in fact it savors of both the genius and the style of Origen throughout. For although Hilary's work imparts much excellent instruction clearly revealing the author's expert knowledge of Holy Scripture, nevertheless his allegories are rather far-fetched in several instances and sometimes rather harsh, and his excessive preoccupation with allegorizing results in the loss of the historical sense. It is as if there is no place for allegorizing without impairing the historical sense. Sometimes in joining the two (for he also gives his attention to this) he has amused himself, it seems, with his cleverness rather than treated a serious subject. We see, however, that among his innumerable gifts this failing is peculiar to Origen in nearly all his writings. I wish that the man had many imitators of his other qualities as he had some followers even among Latin authors in this aspect of his work. Furthermore Jerome declares that the commentaries which he published on the Psalms were more truly imitations of Origen's commentaries than translations, especially since he himself had made some contributions of his own. What these are the experienced reader will have no difficulty perceiving, for they are by and large the ideas which he had advanced in so many books against the Arians. He himself does not indicate anywhere whom he has followed; however, I think he did this not to conceal his benefactor but to avoid the odium attaching to Origen's name. Ambrose does the same thing everywhere.

Jerome mentions this work in the preface of the second book on Micah. He cites Hilary as having paraphrased nearly forty thousand lines from Origen on the Psalms. One wonders, however, what Hilary's plan was in selecting certain Psalms for translation and passing over the rest, unless by chance it was because he did not happen to come upon the complete work of Origen. He wrote, as Jerome recounts, on the first and second Psalm, then on the fifty-first to the sixty-second, and again on the hundred and eighteenth to the last. But we have more than the number Jerome gives —namely, besides the first two we have commentaries from the fifty-first Psalm to the sixty-ninth and again from the hundred and eighteenth Psalm to the end, except that the last part appears to be missing in the copies. This happened, I suspect, because the final page of the manuscript codices had been either torn off or had worn out. That page as a rule is lost like the last bean plant in the proverb.[37] It is inferred from this that Hilary's work on the Psalms did not reach Jerome in its entirety. For he published the *Catalogus* of famous writers after the death of Hilary, so no one can claim that Hilary made certain additions to his work after Jerome published his *Catalogus*. And he testifies in this connection that he heard from some persons that Hilary had written commentaries on the Song of Songs, but he denies that he had seen this work.

Many works indeed have been lost to us, namely, letters which he wrote to various persons and also a book of hymns. For an extant letter to his daughter Apra has nothing of Hilary and a hymn has far less and not even the character of a song, although Jerome testifies somewhere that he wrote that song. Nevertheless, we have included both to provide a sample for anyone who by chance might wish to make a judgment on these matters. The literary style and composition of Hilary show that he was not infelicitous in writing verse, and perhaps several hymns which the Church sings today, not without art but of uncertain authorship, are his, as for example the hymn *De ligno crucis* which begins "Crux fidelis" and the hymn *De Ioanne Baptista* which begins "Ut queant laxis."[38] We also lack the commentaries on Job which, as Jerome in the same work declares, he paraphrased from Origen. And indeed there is extant among the remains of Origen a commentary on Job, the style of which has no affinity with Hilary's. In fact the preface testifies that this same work had been translated by some others but with neither accuracy nor learning. They made bad Latin out of good Greek. The author of the preface himself in reality makes clear that he was a man who neither knew Latin nor had talent or learning but whose presumptuousness matched his ignorance. We are also lacking that book which he wrote against the prefect Sallustius or against Dioscorus the physician. In it he displayed, it seems, all the powers of his talent and eloquence. St. Jerome makes this point in a letter to the orator Magnus: "In a brief essay which he wrote against Dioscorus the physician he has shown his literary power."[39] Also missing is a book against Valens and Ursacius which contains a history of the Council of Rimini and the acts of the Council of Seleucia, unless by chance this work was added to *De Synodis*.[40]

So much for the discussion of the individual works of our author. Now we shall offer a few remarks in general about the gifts of this most praiseworthy man. But first what point is there in speaking about the sanctity of his life when ecclesiastical authority has long since inscribed his name in the catalogue of saints? In any event, however, all his books breathe what I might call a wonderful fervor of holiness. How great the authority attaching to his name was may be surmised even from the fact that St. Jerome who came close to belittling Augustine and who did not regard Ambrose too highly often cites Hilary with great veneration, calling him in one place "the Deucalion of the world,"[41] in another "a trumpet of the Latin language," and in another "the Rhône of Latin eloquence." And in more than one passage Jerome made use of the example of that man like a shield against those who falsely charged him with consorting with the Origenists, and he accorded him the fullest testimonial in a letter to Marcella, when he says: "I do not dare criticize so great a man, the most eloquent of his day, who is praised for his meritorious service as a witness as well as for the industry which marked his life and the clarity which characterized his eloquence wherever the name of Rome has reached."[42] What statement covers more ground than this? And Jerome mentions him with no less respect in his Commentary on Isaiah, when he says: "Do not Cyprian, a holy and most eloquent martyr, and Hilary, a confessor of our time, seem to you to be like lofty trees, the kind we find once in a lifetime, in the building of the Church of God?" Indeed St. Augustine also by way of introduction cites not without praise the authority of Hilary in his *De Trinitate*.

On the other hand Hilary was entirely untrained in Hebrew. Hence if he dealt with anything in this language either he used Origen as a source or he handled it with little success. Indeed in explaining a Psalm he suggests that *Bresith* is more correctly rendered by *in filio* than by *in principio*—so Jerome reports in his notes on *The Traditions of the Hebrews on Genesis*—yet the authority of the Septuagint stands in clear opposition to this, as do Symmachus and Theodotion who fully concur in the translation ἐν ἀρχῇ.[43] It is also at odds with the Hebrew text itself which has *Bresith* and which Aquila takes to mean ἐν κεφαλίδι—that is, *in capitulo*. It does not have *Babem* which is the translation of *in filio*. The word "head," however, is also used for the beginning of anything. In this instance no one may rightly ask for consistency in Hilary who, although he highly praises in more than one passage the authority of the Septuagint from which he thinks it wrong to depart a hair's breadth, as it were, has not hesitated to disagree on this word. I suspect that the passage which Jerome alludes to is in the commentary which Hilary wrote on the second Psalm, for there he notes in passing that *Bresith* in Hebrew has three meanings: *in principio*, *in capite*, and *in filio*. Although this word has been rendered in different ways by translators Jerome thinks that there must be no deviation from the authority of the Septuagint. But Hilary made an even more extraordinary mistake with the term *Hosanna*. In his commentary on Matthew he states that the word in Hebrew means *sanctificatio domus David*, although there is nothing in this term which has any affinity with such an interpretation. Indeed in Hebrew *redemptio* is *Pheduth*, and *domus* is *Beth*. Moreover, it is self-evident to all that *David*, since it is the same word in Latin, Greek, and Hebrew, was not inserted here, as Jerome somewhere informs us.

Furthermore he had studied Greek literature superficially, if indeed we believe Jerome whose comment on this I quote from the letter to Marcella wherein he explains the one hundred and twenty-sixth Psalm.

However, he should not be blamed [he writes], ignorant of Hebrew as he was and with only a smattering of Greek, but the priest Heliodorus with whom he was intimately associated should be blamed. He used to ask him what Origen meant by those words he could not understand. Heliodorus, since he could not find Origen's commentary on this Psalm, was not reluctant to insinuate his own opinion rather than to admit his ignorance, and Hilary adopted it and discussed it in clear language and with some eloquence set forth the error of another.[44]

So far we have reviewed the words of Jerome in which while he zealously defends Hilary he treats Heliodorus with repugnance, especially since his explanation is only conjectural. But at this point to defend Hilary in passing, it is not likely, I think, that such a great man was so credulous that in expounding Holy Scripture he placed his total reliance on the judgment of another or that he was so deficient in his knowledge of Greek literature that he could not of himself grasp the meaning of the original, especially in the case of Origen whose language is admirably clear. This we can easily infer from those works surviving in a Latin translation. Yet I do not quite see what caused the displeasure of St. Jerome here. For the fact that he gives various translations from the Hebrew by ancient scholars has no bearing on Hilary who admittedly always follows the Septuagint version which in this passage has the translation $\dot{\epsilon}\kappa\tau\epsilon\tau\iota\nu\alpha\sigma\mu\dot{\epsilon}\nu\omega\nu$.[45]

Moreover, St. Jerome asserts that Hilary interpreted the phrase "the sons of those shaken off" to mean the Apostles because they were ordered to shake the dust off their feet with reference to those who had not accepted the Gospel.[46] But if anyone should read with some attention Hilary's commentary on the Psalm *Unless the Lord build the house* he will find that the case is somewhat different. For in my opinion Hilary calls those who through their own fault have been rejected by God and have been "shaken off" as accursed because of their stubborn disbelief "the apostles and prophets of those shaken off"—that is, "the sons of the wicked." But his passing mention in two words of the dust shaken from the feet means not that the Apostles are said to be "shaken off" but that the dust shaken off in the case of the disbelieving Jews signifies that because of their stubborn rejection of the grace of the Gospel they themselves have been "shaken off" for the falsity of their understanding. This he also explains more clearly in his Commentary on Matthew in the words: "And by the sign of the dust shaken off the feet let an everlasting curse be left behind." I might also refer to the words of Hilary himself from the Psalms except that it would be tedious and irksome for the reader, especially in a preface. The fact is, then, that here Jerome either had a lapse of memory or had not read Hilary's commentary with enough attention. Now when Jerome approves the comment of Marcella who wrote that the Apostles were "the sons of those shaking off" rather than "of those shaken off," I for my part do not see what he means, unless perhaps as the Greeks speak of "sons of doctors" for "doctors" so the Apostles were called "the sons of those shaken off" for "the shaken off." Otherwise the successors of the Apostles ought rather to have been called "the sons of those shaken off," if the Apostles are correctly known by the name of "the shaken off." Yet it is not absurd for those who have shaken themselves off to be called "the shaken off," just as those who have washed themselves are called washed and those who have dined are called the dined. For so it is that both the dust has been shaken off and the man or his foot shaken off, as we say something that stains has been spattered on a man and a man has been spattered by something that stains.

It seemed appropriate to touch on these matters in passing not only to defend Hilary, but also to show that at one time the holiest men had no scruples about disagreeing with authors however great, and further that even the greatest men sometimes nod, as did Jerome in this instance in criticizing Hilary. Each man is a friend, but the truth ought to be the greater friend for everyone.[47]

Let us now return to the original point. I would readily believe all the same that Hilary did not have a complete knowledge of Greek literature. For as far as elegance of style is concerned he is more exuberant in what he writes of and by himself than in what he translates, for his translations are more concise and restrained in thought. I suspect that the cause of this was his practice not to undertake to translate anything unless he was free to use his own discretion in rendering the meaning and to omit or add what he thought proper. This is the safer course for anyone who does not have full command of the language he is translating. Poggio availed himself of the same privilege in translating Diodorus Siculus, Rufinus did the same in almost everything he translated especially in the case of the books of Origen and the history of Eusebius of Caesarea. Even so this is not the liberty of the translator but rather the license which contaminates the writings of another. Hilary, however, never professed to be a translator save in De Synodis, any more than did Ambrose who for the most part drew upon the works of Origen in his writings. It is my opinion that as the Greek text presented itself to him he erred when in assigning attributes to each Person of the Trinity he ascribes Eternity to the Father, Image to the Son, and Use to the Holy Spirit.[48] Perhaps he read in Greek τὸ χρῆστον or χρηστότητα which is derived from the Greek ἀπὸ τοῦ χρῆσθαι—that is, "from using." From this εὔχρηστος means friendly and suitable to everyday life, and ἄχρηστος means useless. But χρῆστον or χρηστότης in Greek has to do not with use or utility so much as with goodness, friendliness, agreeableness, or, a frequent translation, kindness. Power is attributed to the Father, Wisdom to the Son, and Goodness to the Holy Spirit. Augustine cites this passage in his *De Trinitate*, going to some trouble in explaining what the term "Use" means.[49]

However this may be, although St. Hilary did not have full command of Greek, it is nevertheless worthwhile to see how carefully he philosophizes about the usage of Greek words in his Commentary on the Psalms, now diligently pointing out their aptness and significance, now seeking the meaning of the Greek not rendered with requisite propriety by the Latin translator, now removing the ambiguity from Latin words with the help of the Greek. And where meanwhile are those who say that Greek literature is of no value in the study of Holy Scripture? Where are those individuals—camels rather than men—who bleat that nothing comes out of Greek literature except heresies? And though they keep shouting out these thoughts in public sermons, they are amazed if some persons think that they are in need of a dose of hellebore. Indeed the translation he uses is different from the one which has now been commonly accepted![50] Moreover, since Cyprian has his own translation, as do Augustine and Ambrose, and Hilary, and Tertullian (his is different from all others), it is quite clear that at one time there was no translation which everyone used.[51]

But indeed I am remarkably shameless in keeping the eager reader from perusing the inspired work by so wordy a preface. I shall come to a close, therefore, after I have made this one request of you, most gracious Prelate. I ask that you accept this work of mine, such as it is, dedicated to your name, as a pledge and memorial of my devotion to you. Let others judge what we have done. At least we have made a great effort to place Hilary, that unique light of Gaul, into the hands of men in a considerably more correct and refined form. The publication of his work will have even greater appeal with the addition of your approval, since your influence is foremost in the opinion of all and your sound and sincere judgments are well known to everyone. Your outstanding abilities are one with the abilities of the Carondelet family which in its abundant fruitfulness has given us many besides the distinguished Chancellor of Burgundy.[52] I have known five of them, men of no less cultivation than integrity, loaded with every kind of honor.

You understand therefore what I am seeking. I am of course seeking to gain from the luster of the Carondelet name some favor for Hilary who ought to be held in the highest esteem by all students of theology. For I see that some in view of the new books which are now springing forth from every quarter are disdainful of the ancient authors, and to such an extent that they think that both Origen and Jerome like sexagenarians in the proverb must be driven from the bridge.[53] Just as men of genius in these times who either invent something new or restore something old should, I think, be above contempt, so it is characteristic of an inferior mind not to accord to old age the honor due it and characteristic also of an ungrateful mind to reject those to whose persevering efforts the Christian world owes so much. For what could we accomplish now in scriptural studies without the aid of the works left us by Origen, Tertullian, Chrysostom, Jerome, Hilary, and Augustine? I do not think that the works of either Thomas or Scotus should be rejected in their entirety. They wrote for their own age, and they passed on to us much that was drawn from the books of the ancient Fathers and examined with some discrimination. But I do not approve of the rudeness of those who ascribe so much to this kind of author that they believe they have the obligation to clamor against good literature happily springing up again everywhere. Diverse are the gifts of men of genius, and many are the different kinds of ages. Let each one reveal the scope of his competence, and let no one be envious of another who in keeping with his own ability and style tries to make a useful contribution to the education of all. Reverence is the due of ancient authors, especially those authors who are recommended by the sanctity of their lives in addition to their learning and eloquence; but this reverence does not exclude a critical reading of them. Fairness is the due of modern authors so that they may be read without ill-will, though not without discrimination. Let the absence of furious contention, the bane of peace and concord, prevail everywhere. And let the Graces whom the ancients not without good reason conceived as the companions of the Muses attend upon our studies.

May He without whom there can be no salvation preserve your Excellency safe for us for a long time, most illustrious Prelate.

Basel. January 5, 1523

NOTES

1. Erasmus' complaints about the liberty of copyists and the corruption of Hilary's text are echoed in P. Smulders, s.j., "Remarks on the Manuscript Tradition of the *De Trinitate* of Saint Hilary of Poitiers," *Studia Patristica*, III, Part 1 (Berlin, 1961), 133–34.

2. *De Trinitate* 10.23.

3. *De Trinitate* 10.47. The reference to this theme in Hilary's *De Trinitate* recalls Erasmus' dispute with John Colet in 1499 on the nature of Christ's agony in the garden of Gethsemane. He upheld the traditional view that Christ in His human nature feared death. He subsequently published a printed version of their exchange under the title of the *Disputatiuncula de tedio, pavore, tristicia Iesu*.

4. Terence, *Phormio*, 186. See also Erasmus' *Adagiorum chiliades*, No. 347.

5. *Sentences* 3.15.5. The four books of the *Sentences* were a basic theological text in the Middle Ages. In the part Erasmus refers to, Peter Lombard discusses certain passages from Hilary.

6. Martial 1, preface.

7. The Cerinthians and Ebionites were early heretical sects, both of which held that Jesus was born as a mere man. Irenaeus asserted that St. John wrote his Gospel to refute the heretic Cerinthus.

8. ὁμοούσιον and ὁμοιούσιον mean "of the same substance" and "of a similar substance," respectively, and were terms used in the controversy in the fourth century over the divinity of Christ.

9. This passage is one which was censured by the Sorbonne in 1526. The *censura* declared that St. Hilary did *not* think it dangerous to make pronouncements which were in conformity with an ecumenical council.

10. Also censured by the Sorbonne as being "contumelious" toward General Councils and the study of the Doctors of the Church.

11. *Odyssey* 4.392.

12. The wise man is Socrates, and Erasmus here and above is echoing what Cicero said of Socrates in *Tusculanae disputationes* 5.4.10.

13. 1 Cor. 8:1. The passage beginning "But those questions" was censured by the Sorbonne which defended the definition of doctrine about the Trinity and denied that this was "knowledge that puffs up."

14. Gal. 5:22. This sentence was censured by the Sorbonne.

15. This sentence has been interpreted as referring to the development of scholastic theology. It was censured by the Sorbonne, and the *censura* defended the value of scholastic theology. Erasmus uses the Greek word θεότητα for what we in this context have termed "system of theology."

16. In his *Ratio verae theologiae* (1518) Erasmus declares that "the chief aim of theologians is to interpret wisely Holy Scripture." LB, V, 83.

17. Cf. 1 Cor. 13:12. The above paragraph was a particularly controversial part of the preface. Five separate statements or propositions from it were censured by the Sorbonne, the sentence beginning "But certain pundits" being one of these. The "pundits" (Erasmus actually uses the term "rabbis") were understood to be scholastic doctors, and the *censura* states that they are ashamed when they see Councils contemned and Holy Scripture twisted *ad haereticum sensum*.

18. Epistle 58.10.

19. See *De Trinitate* 1.18. This last sentence recalls the dictum of Egidio da Viterbo in his opening address to the Fifth Lateran Council in May 1512: "Men must be changed by religion, not religion by men."

20. Both Sulpicius Severus and St. Eucherius were early Christian authors, and both were Gauls, Eucherius being a Bishop of Lyons in the first half of the fifth century. Guillaume Budé whom Erasmus speaks of in the next sentence was his

own contemporary and was one of France's greatest humanist scholars. His *De asse*, published in Paris in 1515, was a treatise on ancient coinage.

21. Epistle 70.5. Quintilian's great work was *Institutiones oratoriae* which like Hilary's *De Trinitate* consisted of twelve books.

22. This story is told in Cicero's *Brutus* 172 and in Quintilian 8.1.2.

23. This last sentence was one of the passages criticized at the Valladolid conference in 1527.

24. Erasmus is echoing Terence's *Quot homines, tot sententiae* (*Phormio* 454).

25. These last sentiments regarding imperial intervention and the use of force are most interesting to consider in view of the times and the person Erasmus is addressing. The entire passage beginning with the words "The teachings of Christ" had at one time been obliterated in the actual copy of the Hilary edition Erasmus sent to Jean de Carondelet: Houghton Library, Harvard University, *fNC5/Er153/ 523h/(A).

26. Epistle 5.2.

27. Auxentius was appointed to the see of Milan by Constantius in 355 and was a major supporter of Arianism in the West.

28. This sentence also came under attack at the Valladolid conference.

29. This sentence too was criticized at Valladolid.

30. The first part of this sentence and the last portion of the preceding one evoked considerable objection at Valladolid.

31. One of the basic issues in the Lutheran controversy was the question of free will. The next year—in 1524—Erasmus was to write and publish his treatise *De libero arbitrio* defending the freedom of the will against Luther's doctrine. He will uphold a very moderate position, neither Pelagian nor Lutheran.

32. A passage which now follows in the 1523 edition (lines 530–69 in Allen) has been omitted in this translation. Erasmus himself omitted it in the revised edition of Hilary's *Opera* in 1535 because in it he had erroneously discussed a reference in St. Jerome to another Hilary than the one he was concerned with.

33. Maevius was an inferior Latin poet who had attacked Virgil.

34. An interesting observation (together with the example he gives regarding papal authority) in view of the then very serious Lutheran controversy! Erasmus felt himself caught in the middle between two warring factions.

35. The Pauline word is the Greek verb "to cut straight," which St. Paul uses in 2 Timothy 2:15.

36. Erasmus refers to the prophecy in Is. 42:3 which is also quoted in Matt. 12:20. He has on several occasions used this example in discussing the approach which one should take to Luther at this time.

37. Erasmus refers to the proverb "Tam perit quam extrema faba" which he found in Festus Pompeius and which he included in his *Adagiorum chiliades* (No. 3372).

38. These two hymns are not by Hilary. The first is the Good Friday *Pange, lingua* by Venantius Fortunatus, the second is by Paulus Diaconus.

39. Epistle 70.5.

40. Valens and Ursacius were Arian leaders in the West. The Councils of Rimini and Seleucia of 359 were dominated by the Arians. Parts of the book Erasmus refers to came to light later and were published in Paris in 1598.

41. This reference in Jerome to Deucalion (a figure in Greek mythology comparable to Noah) actually applies to another Hilary, and Erasmus should have omitted it in his revised edition as he did the passage mentioned in n. 32.

42. Epistle 34.3. Erasmus will quote this letter again below and will continue to discuss its reference to Hilary.

43. The Septuagint is the Greek version of the Old Testament produced by seventy (*septuaginta*) translators in the third and second centuries B.C. Symmachus and Theodotion as well as Aquila who is mentioned in the next sentence all made Greek translations of the Old Testament in the second century of the Christian era. Origen's *Hexapla* sets forth all of these translations in parallel columns. *Bresith* is the Hebrew word which begins Genesis and is rendered *In principio* in Latin or *In the beginning* in English. The Greek ἐν ἀρχῇ is the equivalent of *in principio*.

44. Epistle 34.3. This passage continues the quotation concerning Hilary which Erasmus quoted above. Jerome's letter to Marcella is devoted to explaining certain terms or phrases in Psalm 126, *Nisi Dominus aedificaverit domum* (Unless the Lord build the house), and Jerome refers, as will Erasmus, to Hilary's commentary on it.

45. The passage Erasmus refers to and which Jerome sought to explain in his letter to Marcella is Ps. 126:4 which contains the phrase in the Latin of Hilary's text (as well as of Marcella's) *filii excussorum*. Literally it means "the sons of those shaken off." In the Septuagint the word for *excussorum* is ἐκτετιναγμένων. Jerome criticizes Hilary's explanation of this enigmatic phrase and indicates how other Greek translators have rendered the original Hebrew expression. Erasmus will discuss this question at some length.

46. Matt. 10:14: "If anyone will not receive you or listen to what you say, then as you leave that house or that town shake the dust of it off your feet."

47. This dictum is drawn from Aristotle's *Nicomachean Ethics* 1.6.1096 and was given a wording and usage similar to Erasmus' by Petrarch in *On His Own Ignorance*. See *The Renaissance Philosophy of Man*, edd. Ernst Cassirer et al. (Chicago, 1948), p. 111.

48. Erasmus refers here to Hilary's *De Trinitate* 2.1.

49. St. Augustine's *De Trinitate* 6.10.

50. Erasmus refers somewhat abruptly to the fact that Hilary's Latin text of Scripture differs in its translation of some Greek and Hebrew words from the later Vulgate. The phrase *filii excussorum*, discussed above, is a good example. In the Vulgate text of Psalm 126 the Hebrew in this instance is rendered *filii juventutis*.

51. A passage which now follows in the Latin text (lines 842–88 in Allen) has been omitted. In it Erasmus points out that Hilary used certain Latin words and grammatical forms oddly or incorrectly, and he gives several examples. Since these involve Latin terms, case endings, etc., their translation is not feasible.

52. The Chancellor of Burgundy was Jean de Carondelet's father. He had several sons, five of whom Erasmus knew, as he tells us in the next sentence.

53. The sexagenarians in the proverb are those who because of their age were no longer permitted to vote in ancient Rome. They were driven back from the bridge which led to the voting place. Erasmus includes this proverb in his *Adagiorum chiliades* (No. 437).

BIBLIOGRAPHICAL NOTE

Though I complained in the preface of this book that Erasmus has not always been given his due, there is actually no dearth of literature about him, nor are his own writings difficult to obtain. My complaint referred chiefly to the matter of interpreting or understanding him, but it also included the neglect of some facets or aspects of his life's work. With regard to the latter the lack of attention to his editions of the early Church Fathers as well as to the patristic character of his Christian humanism comes immediately to mind. A bibliography for Erasmus nevertheless can be a very extensive affair. Jean-Claude Margolin's *Douze années de bibliographie érasmienne (1950–1961)* (Paris, 1963), *Quatorze années de bibliographie érasmienne (1936–1949)* (Paris, 1969), and *Neuf années de bibliographie érasmienne (1962–1970)* (Toronto, 1977) afford ample proof.

I shall not give anything extensive here. For a selective list of Erasmus' own writings and of works about him see the Bibliography in CHR. And most biographies of Erasmus contain bibliographies, the one in Roland H. Bainton's fine life, *Erasmus of Christendom* (New York, 1969), being quite comprehensive. The reader, of course, will also find many references to editions of Erasmus' works and to other studies in the essays published herein and in the appended footnotes. Chapter 5 especially comments on some standard and recent work on Erasmus.

A serious bibliography, however, must call attention to the following source collections that are basic:

Opus epistolarum Des. Erasmi Roterodami. Edd. P. S. Allen, H. M. Allen, and H. W. Garrod. 12 vols. Oxford, 1906–1958.

Erasmi Opera omnia. Ed. Johannes Clericus. 10 vols. Leiden, 1703–1706.

Erasmi Opera omnia. Amsterdam, 1969–. This new critical edition will replace the Leiden *Opera.* 8 volumes have so far been published. It will run eventually to approximately 30 volumes.

Collected Works of Erasmus. Toronto and Buffalo, 1974–. This edition will contain the correspondence and writings of Erasmus in English translation. 4 volumes of the correspondence have so far been published. It will run eventually to approximately 40 volumes. The University of Toronto Press which is publishing this enormous project also publishes an annual newsletter, *Erasmus in English*, to provide information about the CWE and Erasmus studies in general.

Several key works of Erasmus are also readily available in modern English editions:

> *The 'Adages' of Erasmus.* By Margaret Mann Phillips. Cambridge, 1964. There is a shortened paperback edition of this under the title *Erasmus on His Times.*

> *The Enchiridion of Erasmus.* Trans. Raymond Himelick. Bloomington, 1963.

> *The Praise of Folly.* Trans. Betty Radice. Introd. A. H. T. Levi. Baltimore, 1971.

> *The Colloquies of Erasmus.* Trans. Craig R. Thompson. Chicago, 1965.

CHR contains several important short pieces, including the apologetic Letter to Martin Dorp of 1515, the *Paraclesis*, the Letter to Paul Volz which prefaced the 1518 edition of the *Enchiridion*, and the Letter to Albert of Brandenburg of October 1519.

I must confess that I do not know of a truly adequate biography. Johan Huizinga's *Erasmus of Rotterdam*, trans. F. Hopman (originally New York, 1924), has something of the status of a standard life, but I find the interpretation unsatisfactory. Margaret Mann Phillips, *Erasmus and the Northern Renaissance* (London, 1949), and Roland H. Bainton, *Erasmus of Christendom*, in my estimation are preferable. In that company I might also mention E. E. Reynolds, *Thomas More and Erasmus* (New York, 1965), James D. Tracy, *Erasmus: The Growth of a Mind* (Geneva, 1972), and J. Kelley Sowards, *Desiderius Erasmus* (Boston, 1975). These works certainly will amplify the picture and supplement the essays in this volume.

INDEX NOMINUM